Two-Part Ron

Resolving the Calvinism vs.
Whosoever Will Puzzle!

Brent Lay

A DEDICATION

to my wife, Penny,

and my children Caroline, Shelby, and Brandon

for their dedicated journey as a young family

through my years of schooling and service,

and to all the faithful followers of Christ

of Englewood Baptist Church

in Jackson, Tennessee,

a church that I have been a part of

for more than 60 years,

beginning as a child and later serving

as a deacon, Sunday school teacher,

and Associate Pastor.

I also dedicate this writing to my five

grandchildren,

Hayes Eli Yoder, Layton Davis Yoder, Ryder Knox Lay

Emma Adalyn Yoder and Lara June Lay.

May they champion the Word of God

all the days of their lives on this earth.

TABLE OF CONTENTS

Preface

As a graduate of Southern Baptist Theological Seminary and Trinity Theological Seminary, I am well aware that this writing presents a new theological perspective for most people. I have the highest regard for those who defend Calvinism and other systematic doctrinal positions. This book is what I contend represents the original and true perspective of God's Word regarding salvation. It deals primarily with the book of Romans. Based up the context of Scripture, I will introduce and maintain that Augustine and his followers "took a wrong turn" in how they understood Paul's writing in the book of Romans. One of the key issues has to do with a huge misunderstanding of the Apostle Paul writing in the first chapter of Romans. This issue transcends the traditional debate about Calvinism verses non-Calvinism.

The goal is to communicate this truth to lay people as well as theologians. This finding of two-part Romans brings resolution to age-old issues of the traditional Calvinism debate.

In 2013, I was diagnosed with cancer. For the thirty years prior, I was far more a practitioner in evangelism and outreach than a student of theology.

As a word of testimony, I realize now that without this illness, I would have not taken the time to study the book of Romans so relentlessly. With a grateful and thankful heart for answered prayers and added days, I share these words.

When I came upon this discovery, I spent several months searching for historical evidence of others who took this position. I say discovery because I first realized this revelation on Thursday, June 6, 2013, about 10:15 in the morning while on vacation in Florida. Recovering from a cancer treatment, I was confined to a condominium overlooking the beach for the week. In reading through the book of Romans for the 28th consecutive time on the sixth consecutive day, I realized for the first time the reality that Paul had written Romans in two parts. He wrote the first eight chapters to the Jews and the later eight chapters to the Gentiles.

The Southern Baptist Convention was to consider a report on Calvinism the next week. With this controversial report being debated, I had prayed for weeks concerning this theological or soteriological standoff. On previous occasions, I had tried to accept Calvinism. For the most part, I concluded like many others that the obvious conflict presented in Scripture with whosoever will and Calvinism was a deep mystery beyond the finite minds of men. Yet, I often found myself pondering as to why God's Word would present such a major conflict.

In my own journey attending Southern Seminary in Louisville, Kentucky, I clearly remember the day I realized how much the great scholars and translators of the Greek text of the New Testament differed in their interpretations. I came to understand that the differences in translations come about primarily because the word-for-word transfer from one language to another language involves subjective choices. The transfer or translation from a word or phrase in one language, such as Greek, to another language, such as English, necessitates that these choices to be made. These subjective choices include consideration of the nuances of the respective language as well as context. This is particularly true when there is an ambiguous antecedent as we find in verse 13 of Romans chapter one. Secondly, scholars must also use their own judgement in determining the original intent of the author. Please keep this subjectivity in mind. Translating and interpreting God's word is not an exact science like we would prefer. Throughout history, mistakes by men concerning translation and interpretation are well-documented. Therefore, a new and valid finding such as Two-Part Romans is rare but very possible. This is of added value when a better understanding reconciles a major conflict in Scripture. God's Word is inerrant and by that definition is to be consistent and congruent.

After much prayer and study, I am totally convinced the finding of Two-Part Romans is truth. After reading this, I think you will agree.

For the Sake of the Kingdom,

Brent Lay

Introduction

Wonderful news! The Calvinism and whosoever will theological positions can be reconciled.

Could it be that the 13th verse of the first chapter of Romans has been misunderstood all these years and should be understood saying as "to you (the Jewish believers) as well as the rest of the Gentiles (those Gentiles yet to be evangelized)?"

Could it be that the pronoun change in the 13th verse of the first chapter of Ephesians substantiates that Paul saw himself, a Jewish believer, as one of the believers of the elect nation of Israel (Jewish remnant) and saw Gentiles as those "in him you also, when you heard the word of the truth, the gospel of your salvation, and believed in him?"

Could it be that some of the saints of the Old Covenant were in the very presence of Jesus during his ministry on earth, and as those who already had a faith relationship with God prior to the arrival of Jesus. And, they were the ones that God had given to

Jesus (as described in the gospel of John)? Were these "given", the ones Jesus knew and promised to keep and raise up on the last day (John 6:39)?"

Yes, yes, yes and yes indeed!

There is a very good reason to why scholars, theologians and philosophers have not been able to resolve the obvious scriptural conflicts of the "Calvinism versus whosoever will" positions in a clear and convincing manner. It is because most of this debate has been based largely upon a huge misunderstanding accepted on the front end, namely that the book of Romans was written to Jews and Gentile believers throughout the entire sixteen chapters.

Scripture has been taken out of context! As this writing will confirm, Paul did indeed write the letter of Romans in a two-part fashion that I refer to as Two-Part Romans. The change of pronouns in the first chapter of Ephesians cannot be ignored or understated. It cannot be denied that the Gospel of John represents a transitional time between the two covenants or testaments. It is very significant that saints of the Old Covenant were indeed in the presence of Jesus! Jesus, being one with the Father, knew exactly who they were. Jesus said, "My sheep know my voice" (John 10:27). They were indeed given by the Father because they had a faith relationship with the Father previous to the ministry of Jesus on earth.

This finding of Two-Part Romans heralds a truth that establishes an even higher standard of inerrancy and infallibility. The consistency and congruency concerning the doctrine of salvation throughout God's Word is of utmost importance. This (2PR) finding also aligns with Paul's assertion that the mystery of the Gospel of Salvation is revealed not concealed! (Ephesians 3:3-6)

Most all of us agree that the Bible is the best commentary of the Bible. The harmony of Scripture carries the greatest weight in the rules of interpretation of Scripture. It is much like solving a puzzle: when it fits, it fits! Context cannot be ignored. Truth is far too important!

By design, this writing embraces "sola scriptura" or makes the primary evidence Scripture alone. Therefore, you will not find footnotes referencing the opinions of man. Millions of pages have been penned over hundreds of years debating the obvious contradictions in Scripture concerning the positions of "Calvinism versus whosoever will," including the invention of extensive terminology describing positions, such as "Amyraldism," "infralapsarian," "supralapsarian," and "Molinism." In a sense, this writing supersedes or transcends all these quandaries. Again, when you apply the Two-Part Romans truth, the issue of Calvinism versus whosoever will is explained and reconciled by Scripture alone, not philosophical conjecture.

For those who say it is absurd or unbelievable that a corrected interpretation could be accepted after all these years, they need to be reminded that John Calvin is actually the "Johnny come lately" since Calvinism is less than 500 years old compared with church history of more than 2,000 years. Even if you attribute the position to Augustine and Luther, one must acknowledge that there is very little historical evidence that a doctrinal position such as Calvinism was advocated during the first 400 years of church history.

Furthermore, Southern Baptists should quickly remember our own history of interpreting Scripture to support slavery was less than 200 years ago.

Two paramount rules for the correct interpretation of Scripture involves always interpreting within the context or the setting of the author and always allowing the harmony or congruency with other Scripture to be given the greatest weight.

This finding is perfectly aligned with both these rules. It allows all Scripture to be in harmony and all the Scripture fits perfectly! This harmony and congruency with all other Scripture represents the highest standard of inerrancy and infallibility of Scripture.

You may say, well, does the finding of Two-Part Romans make that much difference? Yes, it makes a huge difference! Since, I am writing to lay people as well as theologians, I will include below a brief sample of some of the overall differences in the positions of Calvinism and Whosoever Will.

(a) Many Calvinists believe that the Jewish nation of Israel disobeyed and forfeited their position as the chosen people of God. The whosoever will or traditional Baptist position (I will refer to this position as whosoever will as we proceed) generally maintains that God always planned for a new covenant (the coming and resurrection of Jesus Christ) and that purposed, predestined or elected believers (remnant) of the Jewish nation of Israel were always and continue to be a part of God's plan. They were to serve as a light unto all nations or

Gentiles.

(b) Many Calvinists assert that God has preselected or predestined individuals and that they are born again, made new or regenerated prior to their belief and trust in Jesus as their Savior. Those of the whosoever will position maintain that all who call upon the Lord Jesus Christ shall be saved and that believing precedes the saving or being regenerated as Paul said in Romans 13:10, "For whosoever calls upon the name of the Lord shall be saved." Unlike the Calvinism or Reformed Theology position, the whosoever will position holds that God's grace provides for all people the capacity to call upon the name of the Lord. Furthermore, that whenever any person sincerely calls upon the Lord in true confession and repentance, that person shall be saved.

(c) Most Calvinists do promote missions, but many see missions as seeking and finding those God has preselected. Those of Whosoever Will persuasion generally see missions as sharing the Good News to all people because each and every person has the capacity to be saved. Most Calvinists see heaven or hell as a done deal for every individual before they were born.

(d) Many Calvinists call on all people to believe in

God and see it as the duty of all people to respond to God while they contend that of all those believing, only those preselected or predestined before they were born will truly be saved. Those of the Whosoever Will persuasion believe that all who call upon the name of the Lord will truly be saved.

(e) Many Calvinists assert that God preselected some people to be saved and that all other people have no chance of spending eternity in heaven. They maintain this view portrays the sovereignty and the grace of God. The proponents of the Whosoever Will position generally hold that this view is contrary to the nature of a loving God that "gave his only begotten Son that whoever will believe shall have everlasting life." Some of these same proponents generally see this as an even higher degree of sovereignty and grace in that God stays true to his promises to all who believe and trust him. And, that God predetermined or predestinated the path (by faith), the people originally given the message (the nation of Israel), and their purpose (to bring light unto the Gentiles).

As a first point of clarification, Calvinism is usually considered Reformed Theology. Reformed Theology, however, is broader in scope and technically includes any system of belief that traces its roots back to the

Protestant Reformation. In this writing, I will use the term Calvinism position in contrast to the Whosoever Will position.

As a second point of clarification, we all stand indebted to John Calvin as one of the great leaders of the protestant reformation. As a prolific writer of theology, his writings continue to impact the world. His contributions in the areas of governing and operation of the church, separation of church and state, education for all, free enterprise and capitalism cannot be denied. The issue of this writing concerns the correct interpretation of Romans relating to doctrine of salvation which differs with only a portion of Calvin's teachings.

Beyond one's belief system concerning the doctrine of salvation or systematic as some refer, I contend that a person's position on this issue has huge implications in how that person practices evangelism. I have served in ministry roles in charge of evangelism and outreach in local churches for more than 30 years. This included training and leading people to consider all encounters with other people as opportunities to witness. As I meet new people, I find myself praying before, during and after our conversation. My prayers and thoughts revolve around the question of that person's salvation.

If a person believes that all people who will be saved are saved regardless of witness of others, I am convinced that the zeal for personal evangelism for most people is not the same. Many a cold, rainy night I felt compelled to give my best effort to witness because I believed heaven or hell for someone could weigh in the balances. Therefore, I believe one's theology drives their methodology or their practice in witnessing to others. The finding of Two-Part Romans and the reconciliation of this issue makes a huge difference!

As a Calvinist or as a non-Calvinist, I pray you approach this writing and the related Scripture with an open mind and open heart allowing the Holy Spirit to guide your thinking. "Jesus Christ is the same yesterday, today and forever" (Hebrews 13:8 KJV).

Chapter I.

The Importance of Two-Part Romans:
Resolving the Calvinism vs. Whosoever Will Puzzle!

Paul's letter to the Romans has Two-Parts: chapter 1-8 "to the Jews first" and chapters 9-16 "then to the Gentiles." I use the abbreviation "2PR" for "Two-Part Romans" to refer to this finding.

Yes, Augustine, Luther, Calvin, and even today McArthur, Piper and Grudem interpret chapters 1-8 of Romans to be written to the Gentiles. No question Romans was written to the Jews and the Gentiles.

Few understand however, that Paul wrote directly to the Jews in the first eight chapters and then directly to the Gentiles in the last eight chapters. It is just like Paul said, "...first to the Jews and then to the Gentiles." What difference does it make? A great difference in that the first eight chapters include the teaching of predestination, foreknowledge, and election which apply only to the Jewish believers (remnant).

It is as if Paul is addressing both groups "within the room," but speaks directly to the Jewish believers first and then to the Gentiles. When we interpret otherwise, we confuse and confound the wonderful gospel message and have to explain the obvious contradiction of predestination with whosoever will. Paul was seeking to explain not mystify. As the reformers cried, "Sola Scriptura" or Scripture Alone as the standard, this writing strives to present the evidence primarily from the Scripture itself.

Volumes have been written for hundreds of years interpreting the book of Romans. Augustine, Luther and Calvin interpreted the chapters 1-8 as having been written primarily to Gentile believers. We all agree with Paul's own claim as the apostle to the

Gentiles. (Romans 11:13) (Galatians 2:7-8) (Ephesians 3:1-2)   However, we all know, as a practice, <u>Paul always went to the Jewish synagogues first</u>. (Acts 17:2)

Through the years, theologians have wrongly assumed Paul wrote first and primarily to the Gentile believers in Rome.   Secondly, they have wrongly interpreted a key verse in terms of recipients, that of Romans 1:13. Their interpretation was most likely an honest mistake, but one which has confused the doctrine of salvation for hundreds of years. It must be mentioned that their honest mistake may have been influenced by their bias against Jews which is well documented by their own writings. Augustine's bias is documented in his famous sermon, *"Against the Jews"* and Luther's bias is documented in his book, *"On the Jews and Their Lies"* written in 1543.

There is little to no evidence that the earliest church fathers of the first 400 years of church history ever held to a predestined view as that of Calvin.   As Calvinist Loraine Boettner stated in his book, *"The Reformed Doctrine of Predestination"* page 365, speaking of the early church fathers prior to the fourth century, "Predestination was not made a matter of special study....they assumed that man had full power to accept or reject the gospel."

Perhaps a case can be made that the earliest indication of this error may be traced as far back as 130 A.D. in the writing of Justin Martyr. He wrote, "Christians are the true Israel." (Justin Martyr, Dialogues, Chapter CXXIII, 130 AD) This teaching holds the view that the Church has replaced Israel and that there is no long-term fulfillment of prophecy for the believing remnant of Israel. This view maintains there is no literal millennial kingdom, no restoration of the believing Jews, and no promises fulfilled to the Jewish elect or chosen nation separate from the believing Gentiles. Much of this view is supported by quoting scripture from the first eight chapters of Romans as if Paul was addressing the Gentile believers. This represents a monumental error.

With the magnitude of the importance of your personal verdict in mind, the approach of this writing is as presenting a case in the courtroom of the highest stakes. Evidence piece by piece is presented to be weighed and thoroughly examined. In Chapter II, the points of relevance to which most of us can agree about this issue are stated. In Chapter III, key verses in Chapters 1-8 of Romans are provided within their context. Commentary is deliberately brief as to allow the Scripture and the Holy Spirit to be your utmost guide. Chapter IV provides key verses in Chapters 9-16 of Romans. In Chapter V, the great theological implications are explained. And, in Chapter VI, the question "Is this finding consistent or in harmony with other Scripture?" is answered. Chapter VII explains the theological viewpoint of consistent fulfillment as result of this finding Chapter IX reflects on the question as why the Calvinism view of Andrew Fuller has become so popular with many Baptists. Finally, Chapter IX includes points of summation.

Chapter II.

Starting with Points of Relevance to Which Most of Us Agree:

1. **Agree or Disagree?** It is possible that Augustine (345-430) and Luther (1483-1546) were biased against the Jews as indicated by their own writings.

2. **Agree or Disagree?** Paul expresses his desire for all to understand the mystery of the gospel (Romans 16:25-26) (Ephesians 3:1-5) and instructs Timothy to "think over what I say, for the Lord will give you understanding in everything". (2 Timothy 2:7)

3. **Agree or Disagree?** In Acts 21, Paul indicates he is very concerned about the growing tension between the Jewish believers and the Gentile believers.

4. **Agree or Disagree?** Paul maintains a pattern in his writings of addressing a primary issue or issues before the church in each of his letters.

5. **Agree or Disagree?** Tradition holds that the church or churches in Rome were started by those attending Pentecost who were primarily Jewish. (Acts 2:5)

6. **Agree or Disagree?** The letter of Romans, which was delivered by Phoebe (Acts 16:1-3) and scribed by Terticus (Acts 16), included greetings to more than 20 Jewish recipients. (Rom.16:3-15) including Aquila and Priscilla. Aquila and Priscilla were close friends of Paul and had returned to Rome. (Acts 18:1-3). Most

agree that this list in Chapter 16 of Romans represents at least 24 individuals.

7. **Agree or Disagree?** Historical evidence indicates that the Jewish believers had been expelled from Rome by the Emperor Claudius because of a disruption within the church. At least a portion of the Jews had returned upon the death of Claudius by the time of Paul's writing to the church at Rome, including Aquila and Priscilla (Acts 18:1-3).

8. **Agree or Disagree?** In the Old Testament, Scripture foretells the disbelief of a majority of the people of Israel with only a portion or a remnant (Ezekiel 6:8, Isaiah 10:20-21), a tenth (Isaiah 6:13), a holy seed (Isaiah 6:13), or a stump (Isaiah 11:1) of Israel believing. This disbelief of a majority of the people of Israel was not a surprise to God.

9. **Agree or Disagree?** At the time Paul was writing the letter of Romans he was in Greece,

staying in the house of Gaius, also known as Titus Justus. This time parallels the twentieth chapter of Acts which means that Paul dictated Romans in the midst of Jewish persecution and knowledge of a personal death plot.

10. **Agree or Disagree?** Even though Paul was continuously ridiculed and persecuted by the Jews as he describes in 2 Corinthians 11:24, he never disclaimed his heritage as a Jew of Jews. (Philippians 3:5)

11. **Agree or Disagree?** As stated throughout the Old Testament, Israel is always described as God's chosen people with such examples of scripture as: (a) Exodus 22:4, "Israel is My son, even My firstborn." (b) Deuteronomy 7:6, "For you are a people Holy to the Lord your God. The Lord your God has chosen you to be a people for his treasured possession, out of all the peoples on the face of this earth." (c) Psalm 135:4 "For the Lord hath chosen Jacob unto himself, and Israel for his peculiar treasure."

12. **Agree or Disagree?** Paul, being close friends with Aquila and Priscilla, had first-hand knowledge of the tension between the Jewish and Gentile believers in Rome and knew that this divide was a grave threat to the church. This represents a great motive for Paul to encourage reconciliation in his writing to the church in Rome in order for this church to avoid even more divide and disruption.

13. **Agree or Disagree?** In the book of Romans, Paul refers to the Old Testament as many as 84 times. This indicates that Paul was emphasizing that the work of Christ fulfilled the promises of God in the Old Testament.

14. **Agree or Disagree?** When Paul wrote Romans, he said he was hoping to travel to Rome on his way to Spain, but first he planned to take a gift from the Greek churches to Jerusalem. (Romans 15:25-28)

15. **Agree or Disagree?** An ambiguous antecedent is a pronoun which has two or more possible antecedents (person, place or thing represented by a pronoun) as illustrated in the four examples which follow:

The Pastor dropped his Bible on the chest and it broke open. (what is the it?)

He raised his hands and then the Worship Leader began to sing. (Who is the he?)

The Youth Pastor intended to speak to you as well as the rest of the parents. (Who is/are the you?)

"that I may reap some harvest among you as well as the rest of the Gentiles" (Romans 1:13b ESV). (Who is/are the you?)

With these fifteen points in mind, the next two chapters will establish that Paul wrote Romans to both the Jews and the Gentiles. He spoke to each party directly speaking first to the Jews in chapters 1-8 and then to the Gentiles in chapters 9-15. He wrote to the Jewish believers first and then to the Gentile believers.

Chapter III.

Key Verses of Romans in Chapters 1-8

This chapter establishes the fact that Paul wrote the first eight chapters of Romans directly to the Jewish believers. He is explaining to them that the new covenant is not leaving them out of God's plan. The Scriptural evidence presented in this chapter reveals that Paul is encouraging the Jewish believers to see themselves and the new Gentile believers as one in Christ as always planned by God.

Scripture in the King James Version is provided in italics for your reference to assist your study of these key verses within their context. Use of brief comments and underline are mine for clarification and emphasis. Other quoted translations are indicated by the abbreviations: NIV, ESV, HCSB, RSV or NAS.

Chapter 1.

[1] Paul, a servant of Jesus Christ, called to be an apostle, separated unto the gospel of God, [2] (Which he had promised afore by his prophets in the holy scriptures,)

1. **Vs 1&2 "called to be an apostle set apart...which he promised beforehand through his prophets in the Holy Scriptures" (ESV) By beginning with his qualifications, Paul alludes to the <u>importance of his distinctive Jewish heritage and his calling</u>.**

[3] Concerning his Son Jesus Christ our Lord, which was made of the seed of David according to the flesh;[4] And declared to be the Son of God with power, according to the spirit of holiness, by the resurrection from the dead:[5] By whom we have received grace and apostleship, for obedience to the faith among all nations, for his name:

2. **Vs. 5 "we received grace and apostleship to call all the Gentiles to the obedience that comes from faith for his name sake"**

(NIV) Note that Paul is <u>not</u> speaking to the Gentiles in first person, but instead he begins <u>speaking about the Gentiles</u>. This is a clear indication that he begins his writing speaking to the Jewish believers. Paul did <u>not</u> say, "we received grace and apostleship <u>to call you</u> to obedience."

[6] Among whom are ye also the called of Jesus Christ

3. **Vs. 6, Paul says "<u>among whom are ye also</u> the called of Jesus Christ." (KJV) Obviously, in Paul's mind there was a group among the Gentiles who were "called" that he considered separate and distinct from the Gentile believers. Considering the context, these "also the called" must be the Jewish believers.**

[7] To all that be in Rome, beloved of God, called to be saints: Grace to you and peace from God our Father, and the Lord Jesus Christ.[8] First, I thank my God through Jesus Christ for you all, that your faith is spoken of throughout the whole world.[9] For God is my witness, whom I serve with my spirit in the gospel of his Son, that without ceasing I make

mention of you always in my prayers;[10] Making request, if by any means now at length I might have a prosperous journey by the will of God to come unto you.[11] For I long to see you, that I may impart unto you some spiritual gift, to the end ye may be established;[12] That is, that I may be comforted together with you by the mutual faith both of you and me.[13] Now I would not have you ignorant, brethren, that oftentimes I purposed to come unto you, (but was let hitherto,) that I might have some fruit among you also, even as among other Gentiles.

4. **Vs. 13b "that I might have a harvest among you, just as I have had among the other Gentiles" (NIV) or "that I may reap some harvest among you as well as the rest of the Gentiles." (NAS) Theologians have traditionally interpreted this verse as the basis for Paul's speaking to the Gentiles as well as the Jews throughout this letter. But, this verse contains an ambiguous antecedent and the context of the entire chapter substantiates that Paul is saying in verse 13, "that I may reap some harvest among you (the Jews) as well as the rest of the Gentiles (the rest being those Gentiles in Rome whom had**

not believed compared to the Gentiles he had already evangelized in other places) The correct interpretation or application of this verse is key to understanding that Paul is writing to the Jewish believers throughout the first eight chapters. From this verse forward until chapter 9, Paul is very consistent in referring to the Jews in first person.

[14] I am debtor both to the Greeks, and to the Barbarians; both to the wise, and to the unwise.[15] So, as much as in me is, I am ready to preach the gospel to you that are at Rome also.

5. **Vs. 14-15 "I am obligated both to the Greeks and non- Greeks...I am so eager to preach also to you" (NIV) Paul is saying beyond my obligation to preach to the Greeks or Gentiles, I am so eager to preach to you also. This "you" has to be the Jews. This is another indication that he is addressing the Jews not Gentiles in this part of the letter.**

[16] For I am not ashamed of the gospel of Christ: for it is the power of God unto salvation to everyyone that believeth; to the Jew first, and also to the Greek.

6. Vs 16 "to everyone who believeth, to the Jew first and also to the Greek" (KJV) Paul continues to make a great effort to clearly distinguish the Greek or Gentiles separately from the Jews. Why? Most theologians agree that the Jews have a priority over Gentiles as the (a) chosen people of God (b) guardians of the Old Testament Scriptures (c) people to whom the Messiah himself first came as a Jew to the Jews (Jesus said in John 4:22 that salvation is from the Jews). This speaking to the Jews first <u>is very consistent with the pattern of Paul always going to the Jews first when he brought the gospel to a new place (Acts 17:1-2).</u> Considering the context of Paul's firsthand knowledge of the tension between the Jewish and Gentile believers, it is the major reason Paul is writing to the church at Rome.

[17] For therein is the righteousness of God revealed from faith to faith: as it is written, The just shall live by faith.[18] For the wrath of God is revealed from heaven against all ungodliness and unrighteousness of men, who hold the truth in unrighteousness;[19]

Because that which may be known of God is manifest in them; for God hath shewed it unto them.[20] For the invisible things of him from the creation of the world are clearly seen, being understood by the things that are made, even his eternal power and Godhead; so that they are without excuse:[21] Because that, when they knew God, they glorified him not as God, neither were thankful; but became vain in their imaginations, and their foolish heart was darkened.

7. **Vs 21 "they knew God, they glorified him not as God" (HCSB). Paul is definitely referring to the people of the past who knew God: the Jews. It was not the Gentiles who knew God throughout Old Testament history.**

[22] Professing themselves to be wise, they became fools,[23] And changed the glory of the uncorruptible God into an image made like to corruptible man, and to birds, and four-footed beasts, and creeping things.[24] Wherefore God also gave them up to uncleanness through the lusts of their own hearts, to dishonor their own bodies between themselves: [25] Who changed the truth of God into a lie, and worshipped and served the

creature more than the Creator, who is blessed for ever. Amen.[26] For this cause God gave them up unto vile affections: for even their women did change the natural use into that which is against nature:[27] And likewise also the men, leaving the natural use of the woman, burned in their lust one toward another; men with men working that which is unseemly, and receiving in themselves that recompense of their error which was meet.[28] And even as they did not like to retain God in their knowledge, God gave them over to a reprobate mind, to do those things which are not convenient;[29] Being filled with all unrighteousness, fornication, wickedness, covetousness, maliciousness; full of envy, murder, debate, deceit, malignity; whisperers,[30] Backbiters, haters of God, despiteful, proud, boasters, inventors of evil things, disobedient to parents,[31] Without understanding, covenant breakers, without natural affection, implacable, unmerciful:[32] Who knowing the judgment of God, that they which commit such things are worthy of death, not only do the same, but have pleasure in them that do them.

Chapter 2

[1] Therefore thou art inexcusable, O man, whosoever thou art that judgest: for wherein thou judgest another, thou condemnest thyself; for thou that judgest doest the same things.[2] But we are sure that the judgment of God is according to truth against them which commit such things.[3] And thinkest thou this, O man, that judgest them which do such things, and doest the same, that thou shalt escape the judgment of God?[4] Or despisest thou the riches of his goodness and forbearance and longsuffering; not knowing that the goodness of God leadeth thee to repentance?[5] But after thy hardness and impenitent heart treasurest up unto thyself wrath against the day of wrath and revelation of the righteous judgment of God;[6] Who will render to every man according to his deeds:[7] To them who by patient continuance in well doing seek for glory and honour and immortality, eternal life:[8] But unto them that are contentious, and do not obey the truth, but obey unrighteousness, indignation and wrath,[9] Tribulation and anguish, upon every soul of man that doeth evil, of the Jew first, and also of the Gentile;

8. **Vs 9 "tribulation and anguish upon every soul of man that doeth evil, of the <u>Jew first, and also of the</u> <u>Gentile</u>" (KJV) Paul**

continues to mention the Jew and the Gentile separately as to indicate he is speaking to clarify their differences in some respects and sameness in other respects. He does not want the Jewish believers to misunderstand.

[10] But glory, honour, and peace, to every man that worketh good, to the Jew first, and also to the Gentile:

9. **Vs 10 "to every man that worketh good, to the Jew first, and also the Gentile" (KJV) Obviously, in Paul's mind this distinction and sequence of always listing the Jew first is a very important point in this teaching.**

[11] For there is no respect of persons with God.[12] For as many as have sinned without law shall also perish without law: and as many as have sinned in the law shall be judged by the law; [13] (For not the hearers of the law are just before God, but the doers of the law shall be justified. [14] For when the Gentiles, which have not the law, do by nature the things contained in the law, these, having not the law, are a law unto themselves:

10. **Vs 14 "when the Gentiles which have not the law" (KJV) Paul does not say <u>you</u> Gentiles. This is added evidence that Paul is speaking directly to the Jews about the Gentiles.**

[15] Which shew the work of the law written in their hearts, their conscience also bearing witness, and their thoughts the mean while accusing or else excusing one another;)[16] In the day when God shall judge the secrets of men by Jesus Christ according to my gospel. [17] Behold, thou art called a Jew, and restest in the law, and makest thy boast of God.

11. **Vs 17 "but if you call yourself a Jew and rely on the law and boast in God"(ESV). This is irrefutable evidence that Paul is speaking directly to the Jews in this chapter.**

[18] And knowest his will, and approvest the things that are more excellent, being instructed out of the law;[19] And art confident that thou thyself art a guide of the blind, a light of them which are in darkness,[20] An instructor of the foolish, a teacher of babes, which hast the form of knowledge and of the truth in the law.[21] Thou therefore which

teachest another, teachest thou not thyself? thou that preachest a man should not steal, dost thou steal?[22] Thou that sayest a man should not commit adultery, dost thou commit adultery? thou that abhorrest idols, dost thou commit sacrilege?[23] Thou that makest thy boast of the law, through breaking the law dishonourest thou God?

12. **Vs 23 "Thou that makest thy boast of the law..." Only the Jews made boast of the law. Paul is definitely addressing only the Jews with these verses.**

[24] For the name of God is blasphemed among the Gentiles through you, as it is written.

13. **Vs 24 "for the name of God is blasphemed among the Gentiles through <u>you</u> as it is written" (KJV) (Isa. 52:5) Paul is obviously and undeniably speaking directly to the Jews. Quoting Isaiah 52 is irrefutable evidence.**

[25] For circumcision verily profiteth, if thou keep the law: but if thou be a breaker of the law, thy circumcision is made uncircumcision.[26] Therefore if the uncircumcision keep the righteousness of the law, shall not his uncircumcision be counted for

circumcision?[27] And shall not uncircumcision which is by nature, if it fulfil the law, judge thee, who by the letter and circumcision dost transgress the law?[28] For he is not a Jew, which is one outwardly; neither is that circumcision, which is outward in the flesh:[29] But he is a Jew, which is one inwardly; and circumcision is that of the heart, in the spirit, and not in the letter; whose praise is not of men, but of God.

Chapter 3

[1] What advantage then hath the Jew? or what profit is there of circumcision?

14. **Vs 1 "What advantage then hath the Jew?"** (KJV) **Paul continues to go to great extents to describe the standing of the Jew. Obviously, he is earnestly speaking and appealing to his Jewish brethren of the church in Rome. He does not want them to misunderstand their position in God's plan.**

[2] Much every way: chiefly, because that unto them were committed the oracles of God. [3] For what if some did not believe? shall their unbelief make the

faith of God without effect? [4] God forbid: yea, let God be true, but every man a liar; as it is written, That thou mightest be justified in thy sayings, and mightest overcome when thou art judged. [5] But if our unrighteousness commend the righteousness of God, what shall we say? Is God unrighteous who taketh vengeance? (I speak as a man) [6] God forbid: for then how shall God judge the world? [7] For if the truth of God hath more abounded through my lie unto his glory; why yet am I also judged as a sinner? [8] And not rather, (as we be slanderously reported, and as some affirm that we say,) Let us do evil, that good may come? whose damnation is just. [9] What then? are we better than they? No, in no wise: for we have before proved both Jews and Gentiles, that they are all under sin;[10] As it is written, There is none righteous, no, not one:[11] There is none that understandeth, there is none that seeketh after God.[12] They are all gone out of the way, they are together become unprofitable; there is none that doeth good, no, not one.[13] Their throat is an open sepulchre; with their tongues they have used deceit; the poison of asps is under their lips:[14] Whose mouth is full of cursing and bitterness:[15] Their feet are swift to shed blood:[16] Destruction and misery are in their ways:[17] And the way of peace have they not known:[**18**] There is no fear of God before their eyes.[**19**] Now we know that what things so ever the law saith, it saith to them who are under the law: that every mouth may be stopped, and all the world may become guilty before God.[**20**] Therefore by the deeds of the law there shall no flesh be justified in his sight: for by the law is the knowledge of sin.[**21**] But now the righteousness of God without the law is manifested, being witnessed by the law and the prophets;[**22**] Even the righteousness of God which is by faith of Jesus Christ unto all and upon all them that believe: for there is no difference:[**23**] For all have sinned, and come short of the glory of God;[**24**] Being justified freely by his grace through the redemption that is in Christ Jesus:[**25**] Whom God hath set forth to be a propitiation through faith in his blood, to declare his righteousness for the remission of sins that are past, through the forbearance of God; [**26**] To declare, I say, at this time his righteousness: that he might be just, and the justifier of him which believeth in Jesus.[**27**] Where is boasting then? It is excluded. By what law? of works? Nay: but by the law of faith. [**28**] Therefore we conclude that a man is justified by faith without the deeds of the law. [**29**]

Is he the God of the Jews only? is he not also of the Gentiles? Yes, of the Gentiles also:

15. Vs 29 "Yes, of the Gentiles also" (KJV) Paul is repeating "of the Gentiles" obviously indicating the importance of the distinction to his Jewish brethren.

[30] Seeing it is one God, which shall justify the circumcision by faith, and uncircumcision [31] Do we then make void the law through faith? God forbid: yea, we establish the law.

Chapter 4

[1] What shall we say then that Abraham our father, as pertaining to the flesh, hath found?

16. Vs 1 "What then shall we say was gained by Abraham, our forefather according to the flesh" (ESV) Paul is clearly speaking to the Jews directly by saying "our forefather according to the flesh" in this historical reference.

[2] For if Abraham were justified by works, he hath whereof to glory; but not before God. [3] For what saith the scripture? Abraham believed God, and it

was counted unto him for righteousness.
[4] Now to him that worketh is the reward not
reckoned of grace, but of debt.*[5]* But to him that
worketh not, but believeth on him that justifieth the
ungodly, his faith is counted for righteousness.*[6]*
Even as David also describeth the blessedness of the
man, unto whom God imputeth righteousness
without works, *[7]* Saying, Blessed are they whose
iniquities are forgiven, and whose sins are
covered.*[8]* Blessed is the man to whom the Lord will
not impute sin.*[9]* Cometh this blessedness then upon
the circumcision only, or upon the uncircumcision
also? for we say that faith was reckoned to Abraham
for righteousness.*[10]* How was it then reckoned?
when he was in circumcision, or in uncircumcision?
Not in circumcision, but in uncircumcision.*[11]* And
he received the sign of circumcision, a seal of the
righteousness of the faith which he had yet being
uncircumcised: that he might be the father of all
them that believe, though they be not circumcised;
that righteousness might be imputed unto them
also:*[12]* And the father of circumcision to them who
are not of the circumcision only, but who also walk
in the steps of that faith of our father Abraham,
which he had being yet uncircumcised.*[13]* For the
promise, that he should be the heir of the world, was

not to Abraham, or to his seed, through the law, but through the righteousness of faith. *[14]* For if they which are of the law be heirs, faith is made void, and the promise made of none effect: *[15]* Because the law worketh wrath: for where no law is, there is no transgression.*[16]* Therefore it is of faith, that it might be by grace; to the end the promise might be sure to all the seed; not to that only which is of the law, but to that also which is of the faith of Abraham; who is the father of us all,*[17]* (As it is written, I have made thee a father of many nations,) before him whom he believed, even God, who quickeneth the dead, and calleth those things which be not as though they were.*[18]* Who against hope believed in hope, that he might become the father of many nations; according to that which was spoken, So shall thy seed be. *[19]* And being not weak in faith, he considered not his own body now dead, when he was about an hundred years old, neither yet the deadness of Sara's womb:*[20]* He staggered not at the promise of God through unbelief; but was strong in faith, giving glory to God;*[21]* And being fully persuaded that, what he had promised, he was able also to perform.*[22]* And therefore it was imputed to him for righteousness.*[23]* Now it was not written for his sake alone, that it was imputed to *him;[24] But for us also, to whom it shall be imputed, if we believe on him that raised up Jesus our Lord from the dead; [25] Who was delivered for our offences, and was raised again for our justification.*

Chapter 5

[1] Therefore being justified by faith, we have peace with God through our Lord Jesus Christ:[2] By whom also we have access by faith into this grace wherein we stand, and rejoice in hope of the glory of God.[3] And not only so, but we glory in tribulations also: knowing that tribulation worketh patience;[4] And patience, experience; and experience, hope:[5] And hope maketh not ashamed; because the love of God is shed abroad in our hearts by the Holy Ghost which is given unto us.[6] For when we were yet without strength, in due time Christ died for the ungodly.

17. **Vs 6 "for when <u>we were yet without strength</u>, in due time Christ died for the ungodly" (KJV) The "we" are the Jews before the due time when Christ died. This is clearly referring to the time of Jewish believers as <u>God's people before</u>**

Christic. **Paul is speaking to the Jews and encouraging the Jewish believers about their heritage.**

[7] For scarcely for a righteous man will one die: yet peradventure for a good man some would even dare to die.[8] But God commendeth his love toward us, in that, while we were yet sinners, Christ died for us.[9] Much more then, being now justified by his blood, we shall be saved from wrath through him.[10] For if, when we were enemies, we were reconciled to God by the death of his Son, much more, being reconciled, we shall be saved by his life.

18.Vs 10..."when we were enemies, we were reconciled to God by the death of His Son" KJV This is Paul speaking directly to the Jews who had become the enemies of God prior to the time of Christ. Paul is certainly not speaking to the Gentiles.

[11] And not only so, but we also joy in God through our Lord Jesus Christ, by whom we have now received the atonement.[12] Wherefore, as by one man sin entered into the world, and death by sin; and so death passed upon all men, for that all have sinned:[13] (For until the law sin was in the world: but sin is not imputed when there is no law.[14]

Nevertheless death reigned from Adam to Moses, even over them that had not sinned after the similitude of Adam's transgression, who is the figure of him that was to come.[15] But not as the offence, so also is the free gift. For if through the offence of one many be dead, much more the grace of God, and the gift by grace, which is by one man, Jesus Christ, hath abounded unto many. [16] And not as it was by one that sinned, so is the gift: for the judgment was by one to condemnation, but the free gift is of many offences unto justification. [17] For if by one man's offence death reigned by one; much more they which receive abundance of grace and of the gift of righteousness shall reign in life by one, Jesus Christ.)[18] Therefore as by the offence of one judgment came upon all men to condemnation; even so by the righteousness of one the free gift came upon all men unto justification of life.[19] For as by one man's disobedience many were made sinners, so by the obedience of one shall many be made righteous.[20] Moreover the law entered, that the offence might abound. But where sin abounded, grace did much more abound: [21] That as sin hath reigned unto death, even so might grace reign through righteousness unto eternal life by Jesus Christ our Lord.

Chapter 6

[1] What shall we say then? Shall we continue in sin, that grace may abound? [2] God forbid. How shall we, that are dead to sin, live any longer therein? [3] Know ye not, that so many of us as were baptized into Jesus Christ were baptized into his death? [4] Therefore we are buried with him by baptism into death: that like as Christ was raised up from the dead by the glory of the Father, even so we also should walk in newness of life.[5] For if we have been planted together in the likeness of his death, we shall be also in the likeness of his resurrection:[6] Knowing this, that our old man is crucified with him, that the body of sin might be destroyed, that henceforth we should not serve sin.

[7] For he that is dead is freed from sin. [8] Now if we be dead with Christ, we believe that we shall also live with him:[9] Knowing that Christ being raised from the dead dieth no more; death hath no more dominion over him.[10] For in that he died, he died unto sin once: but in that he liveth, he liveth unto God.[11] Likewise reckon ye also yourselves to be dead indeed unto sin, but alive unto God through Jesus Christ our Lord.[12] Let not sin

therefore reign in your mortal body, that ye should obey it in the lusts thereof.[13] Neither yield ye your members as instruments of unrighteousness unto sin: but yield yourselves unto God, as those that are alive from the dead, and your members as instruments of righteousness unto God.[14] For sin shall not have dominion over you: for ye are not under the law, but under grace.[15] What then? shall we sin, because we are not under the law, but under grace? God forbid.[16] Know ye not, that to whom ye yield yourselves servants to obey, his servants ye are to whom ye obey; whether of sin unto death, or of obedience unto righteousness?[17] But God be thanked, that ye were the servants of sin, but ye have obeyed from the heart that form of doctrine which was delivered you.[18] Being then made free from sin, ye became the servants of righteousness.[19] I speak after the manner of men because of the infirmity of your flesh: for as ye have yielded your members servants to uncleanness and to iniquity unto iniquity; even so now yield your members servants to righteousness unto holiness.[20] For when ye were the servants of sin, ye were free from righteousness.[21] What fruit had ye then in those things whereof ye are now ashamed? for the end of those things is death.[22] But now being made free from sin, and become servants to God, ye have your fruit unto holiness, and the end everlasting life.[23] For the wages of sin is death; but the gift of God is eternal life through Jesus Christ our Lord.

Chapter 7

[1] Know ye not, brethren, (for I speak to them that know the law,) how that the law hath dominion over a man as long as he liveth?

19. Vs. 1 "Know ye not, brethren, (for I <u>speak to them</u> <u>that know the law</u>") (KJV) Without question, Paul is defining "brethren" as the Jews. The Jews were the ones who historically knew the law, not the Gentiles.

[2] For the woman which hath an husband is bound by the law to her husband so long as he liveth; but if the husband be dead, she is loosed from the law of her husband.[3] So then if, while her husband liveth, she be married to another man, she shall be called an adulteress: but if her husband be dead, she is free from that law; so that she is no adulteress, though she be married to another man[4] Wherefore, my brethren, ye also are become dead to the law by the

body of Christ; that ye should be married to another, even to him who is raised from the dead, that we should bring forth fruit unto God.[5] For when we were in the flesh, the motions of sins, which were by the law, did work in our members to bring forth fruit unto death.[6] But now we are delivered from the law, that being dead wherein we were held; that we should serve in newness of spirit, and not in the oldness of the letter.

20. **Vs. 6 "but now we are released from the law, having died to that which held us captive" (ESV) Paul clarifies that the law he speaks of in verse 1 is not just any law, but the law of the Jews. Certainly, the Gentiles were not historically held captive by the law.**

Chapter 8

[1] There is therefore now no condemnation to them which are in Christ Jesus, who walk not after the flesh, but after the Spirit. [2] For the law of the Spirit of life in Christ Jesus hath made me free from the law of sin and death.[3] For what the law could not do, in that it was weak through the flesh, God sending his own Son in the

likeness of sinful flesh, and for sin, condemned sin in the flesh:[4] That the righteousness of the law might be fulfilled in us, who walk not after the flesh, but after the Spirit.[5] For they that are after the flesh do mind the things of the flesh; but they that are after the Spirit the things of the Spirit.[6] For to be carnally minded is death; but to be spiritually minded is life and peace.[7] Because the carnal mind is enmity against God: for it is not subject to the law of God, neither indeed can be.[8] So then they that are in the flesh cannot please God.[9] But ye are not in the flesh, but in the Spirit, if so be that the Spirit of God dwell in you. Now if any man have not the Spirit of Christ, he is none of his.[10] And if Christ be in you, the body is dead because of sin; but the Spirit is life because of righteousness.[11] But if the Spirit of him that raised up Jesus from the dead dwell in you, he that raised up Christ from the dead shall also quicken your mortal bodies by his Spirit that dwelleth in you.[12] Therefore, brethren, we are debtors, not to the flesh, to live after the flesh.

21. **Vs. 12 "therefore, brethren, we are debtors" (KJV)   This is consistent with brethren who Paul had just defined in 7:1, the Jews of the law. Note he does not change pronouns throughout these first**

eight chapters. Paul has consistently spoken directly to the Jewish believers in first person. This cannot be refuted.

[13] For if ye live after the flesh, ye shall die: but if ye through the Spirit do mortify the deeds of the body, ye shall live [14] For as many as are led by the Spirit of God, they are the sons of God. [15] For ye have not received the spirit of bondage again to fear; but ye have received the Spirit of adoption, whereby we cry, Abba, Father.

22. **Vs.15 "for ye have not received the spirit of bondage again in fear" (KJV) Again the "ye" must be Jews as they were the only ones in bondage to the law in the past, not the Gentiles.**

[16] The Spirit itself beareth witness with our spirit, that we are the children of God:[17] And if children, then heirs; heirs of God, and joint-heirs with Christ; if so be that we suffer with him, that we may be also glorified together.[18] For I reckon that the sufferings of this present time are not worthy to be compared with the glory which shall be revealed in us.[19] For the earnest expectation of the creature waiteth for the manifestation of the sons of God.[20] For the creature was made subject to vanity, not

willingly, but by reason of him who hath subjected the same in hope,[21] Because the creature itself also shall be delivered from the bondage of corruption into the glorious liberty of the children of God.[22] For we know that the whole creation groaneth and travaileth in pain together until now.[23] And not only they, but ourselves also, which have the firstfruits of the Spirit, even we ourselves groan within ourselves, waiting for the adoption, to wit, the redemption of our body.

23. **Vs. 23. "but ourselves also, which have the first fruits of the Spirit" (KJV) Paul was consistent in using "ourselves" to refer to all the Jewish believers as the first fruits. The Spirit first came at Pentecost to the Jewish believers. The church began with Jewish believers.**

[24] For we are saved by hope: but hope that is seen is not hope: for what a man seeth, why doth he yet hope for? [25] But if we hope for that we see not, then do we with patience wait for it.

24. **Vs 24-25 "but we are saved by hope... that we see not". (KJV) Paul is speaking**

of the Jews who had faith in God through believing in the coming of Christ before the ministry of Christ on earth. They were saved through faith in Christ who they had not seen. Their faith was on the basis of hope not sight. Gentiles were not the people who historically waited with patience before Christ.

[26] Likewise the Spirit also helpeth our infirmities: for we know not what we should pray for as we ought: but the Spirit itself maketh intercession for us with groanings which cannot be uttered. [27] And he that searcheth the hearts knoweth what is the mind of the Spirit, because he maketh intercession for the saints according to the will of God. [28] And we know that all things work together for good to them that love God, to them who are the called according to his purpose.

25. **Vs 28 "called according to his purpose" (KJV) Paul saw himself and others being strengthened by the Holy Spirit as the called out to bring the gospel to all men. This is consistent with Jeremiah 29, that the purpose of the Jews was to be a light unto the Gentiles.**

[29] For whom he did foreknow, he also did predestinate to be conformed to the image of his Son, that he might be the firstborn among many brethren.

26. **Vs 29 "whom he did foreknow" (KJV) This is supported by Amos 3:1-2, (1b) "<u>O people of Israel... (2a) you only have I known of all the families of the earth</u>". Paul is describing the believers of the foreknown nation of Israel as those God did predestinate to be conformed to the image of the Son that they might be the firstborn of all believers. Paul is clarifying that the plan of God always included the role of Jewish believers as the first of all believers. This represents encouraging words to the Jewish believers of the church of Rome.**

[30] Moreover whom he did predestinate, them he also called: and whom he called, them he also justified: and whom he justified, them he also glorified. [31] What shall we then say to these things? If God be for us, who can be against us? [32] He that spared not his own Son, but delivered him up for us all, how shall he not with him also freely give

us all things? [33] Who shall lay anything to the charge of God's elect? It is God that justifieth.

27. **Vs 33 "Who shall bring any charge against God's elect?" (ESV). In Chapter 11, verse 7, Paul clearly defines God's elect as the people of promise, the Jews, as believers through their faith throughout the ages. So, again, Paul is speaking to the Jews, not the Gentiles, throughout these first eight chapters of Romans. Speaking to the Jews, Paul is defending why some Jews believed and others did not. It was God who justified, or made right his relationship with a portion of the Jews because of their faith just as Abraham. Obviously, this addressed a great question as to why not all of the Jews were included because of their physical heritage as the nation of Israel.**

These 27 exhibits of internal evidence or evidence within the Scripture are consistent and conclusive that Paul is speaking directly to the Jews in Chapters 1-8 of Romans. As you read the next chapter you will see firsthand that in Chapters 9-15, Paul is speaking directly to the Gentiles.

Chapter IV.

KEY VERSES OF ROMANS

IN CHAPTERS 9-16

The key verses and context of these verses provide conclusive evidence that Paul is no longer speaking to the Jews in Chapters 9-16, but he is speaking directly to the Gentiles.

Chapter 9

[1] I say the truth in Christ, I lie not, my conscience also bearing me witness in the Holy Ghost, [2] That I have great heaviness and continual sorrow in my heart. [3] For I could wish that myself were accursed from Christ for my brethren, my kinsmen according to the flesh: [4] Who are Israelites; to whom pertaineth the adoption, and the glory, and the

covenants, and the giving of the law, and the service of God, and the promises;

1. **Vs 3b &4 "For I wish myself were accursed and cut off for the <u>sake of my brethren</u>, my kinsmen according to the flesh. <u>They are Israelites</u>, to whom <u>belong the adoption</u>, the glory, the covenants, the giving of the law, the service of God, and the promises" (ESV) Paul has been consistent in Chapters 1-8 referring to his brethren as the Jews and now clearly defines them as the Israelites. Note at this point, he does not say YOU, but instead says THEY ARE ISRAELITES. <u>CHAPTER 9 REPRESENTS PAUL SWITCHING HIS AUDIENCE. HE NOW IS OBVIOUSLY SPEAKING DIRECTLY TO THE GENTILES</u>. Otherwise, Paul would have said, "you my brethren".**

[5] Whose are the fathers, and of whom as concerning the flesh Christ came, who is over all, God blessed forever Amen. [6] Not as though the word of God hath taken none effect. For they are not all Israel, which are of Israel:[7] Neither, because

they are the seed of Abraham, are they all children: but, In Isaac shall thy seed be called. *[8]* That is, They which are the children of the flesh, these are not the children of God: but the children of the promise are counted for the seed.*[9]* For this is the word of promise, At this time will I come, and Sara shall have a son.*[10]* And not only this; but when Rebecca also had conceived by one, even by our father Isaac;*[11]* (For the children being not yet born, neither having done any good or evil, that the purpose of God according to election might stand, not of works, but of him that calleth) *[12]* It was said unto her, The elder shall serve the younger.*[13]* As it is written, Jacob have I loved, but Esau have I hated.*[14]* What shall we say then? Is there unrighteousness with   God? God forbid.*[15]* For he saith to Moses, I will have mercy on whom I will have mercy, and I will have compassion on whom I will have compassion.*[16]* So then it is not of him that willeth, nor of him that runneth, but of God that sheweth mercy.*[17]* For the scripture saith unto Pharaoh, Even for this same purpose have I raised thee up, that I might shew my power in thee, and that my name might be declared throughout all the earth.*[18]* Therefore hath he mercy on whom he will have mercy, and whom he will he hardeneth. *[19]*

Thou wilt say then unto me, why doth he yet find fault? For who hath resisted his will? [20] Nay but, O man, who art thou that repliest against God? Shall the thing formed say to him that formed it, why hast thou made me thus? [21] Hath not the potter power over the clay, of the same lump to make one vessel unto honour, and another unto dishonour? [22] What if God, willing to shew his wrath, and to make his power known, endured with much longsuffering the vessels of wrath fitted to destruction: [23] And that he might make known the riches of his glory on the vessels of mercy, which he had afore prepared unto glory, [24] Even us, whom he hath called, not of the Jews only, but also of the Gentiles? [25] As he saith also in Osee, I will call them my people, which were not my people; and her beloved, which was not beloved. [26] And it shall come to pass, that in the place where it was said unto them, Ye are not my people; there shall they be called the children of the living God. [27] Esaias also crieth concerning Israel, Though the number of the children of Israel be as the sand of the sea, a remnant shall be saved.

2. **Vs.27 "Though the children of Israel be as the sand of the sea, <u>only a remnant shall be saved.</u>" (KJV) Paul does not say you, but <u>speaks of</u> the children of Israel**

to the Gentiles. Paul is consistent describing a remnant of Israel saved through faith as foreknown and chosen.

[28] For he will finish the work and cut it short in righteousness: because a short work will the Lord make upon the earth.29] And as Esaias said before, Except the Lord of Sabaoth had left us a seed, we had been as Sodom, and been made like unto Gomorrha. [30] What shall we say then? That the Gentiles, which followed not after righteousness, have attained to righteousness, even the righteousness which is of faith. [31] But Israel, which followed after the law of righteousness, hath not attained to the law of righteousness. [32] Wherefore? Because they sought it not by faith, but as it were by the works of the law. For they stumbled at that stumbling stone; [33] As it is written, Behold, I lay in Zion a stumbling stone and a rock of offence: and whosoever believeth on him shall not be ashamed.

Chapter 10

[1] Brethren, my heart's desire and prayer to God for Israel is, that they might be saved

3. Vs. 1 "Brethren, my heart's desire and prayer to God for Israel is, that they

might be saved" (KJV) <u>Paul speaks of brethren as the Gentiles in first person</u>. He is saying, "they might be saved" so he obviously continues to speak to the Gentiles about "they" the Jews.

[2] For I bear them record that they have a zeal of God, but not according to knowledge. [3] For they being ignorant of God's righteousness, and going about to establish their own righteousness, have not submitted themselves unto the righteousness of God. [4] For Christ is the end of the law for righteousness to everyone that believeth. [5] For Moses describeth the righteousness which is of the law, That the man which doeth those things shall live by them. [6] But the righteousness which is of faith speaketh on this wise, Say not in thine heart, Who shall ascend into heaven? (that is, to bring Christ down from above:) [7] Or, who shall descend into the deep? (that is, to bring up Christ again from the dead.) [8] But what saith it? The word is nigh thee, even in thy mouth, and in thy heart: that is, the word of faith, which we preach;[9] That if thou shalt confess with thy mouth the Lord Jesus, and shalt believe in thine heart that God hath raised him from the dead, thou shalt be saved.[10] For with the heart man believeth unto righteousness; and with the mouth confession is

made unto salvation.[**11**] For the scripture saith, Whosoever believeth on him shall not be ashamed.[**12**] For there is no difference between the Jew and the Greek: for the same Lord over all is rich unto all that call upon him.[**13**] For whosoever shall call upon the name of the Lord shall be saved.[**14**] How then shall they call on him in whom they have not believed? and how shall they believe in him of whom they have not heard? and how shall they hear without a preacher?[**15**] And how shall they preach, except they be sent? as it is written, How beautiful are the feet of them that preach the gospel of peace, and bring glad tidings of good things![**16**] But they have not all obeyed the gospel. For Esaias saith, Lord, who hath believed our report? [**17**] So then faith cometh by hearing, and hearing by the word of God. [**18**] But I say, have they not heard? Yes verily, their sound went into all the earth, and their words unto the ends of the world. [**19**] But I say, did not Israel know? First Moses saith, I will provoke you to jealousy by them that are no people, and by a foolish nation I will anger you.

[**20**] But Esaias is very bold, and saith, I was found of them that sought me not; I was made manifest unto them that asked not after me. [**21**] But to Israel

he saith, all day long I have stretch forth my hands unto a disobedient and gainsaying people.

4. **Vs.21 "But, of Israel he says, all day long I have stretched forth my hands unto a disobedient and contrary people". (ESV) Paul begins and ends this chapter speaking directly to the Gentiles about the Jews.**

Chapter 11

[1] I say then, Hath God cast away his people? God forbid. For I also am an Israelite, of the seed of Abraham, of the tribe of Benjamin. [2] God hath not cast away his people which he foreknew. Wot ye not what the scripture saith of Elias? how he maketh intercession to God against Israel, saying,

5. **Vs.1-2 "I say then, hath God cast away his people? God   forbid. For I am also an Israelite, of the seed of Abraham, of the tribe of Benjamin" Vs. 2 "God hath not cast away <u>his people which he foreknew</u>" (KJV) This is irrefutable evidence that clarifies Paul's use of the term "foreknew" refers to Israelites, the Jews,**

his people. The term foreknew as a verb is used only five times in the New Testament and Paul uses the term here and in just two chapters back, chapter 8:29 (The other places are 1 Peter 1:2 and 1:20 as well as Acts 2:23). <u>Paul is saying this foreknowledge is restricted to "his people" the Israelites</u>. This finding is consistent with Amos 3:1b &2 "O children of Israel, ...You only have I known of all the families of the earth."

[3] Lord, they have killed thy prophets, and digged down thine altars; and I am left alone, and they seek my life. [4] But what saith the answer of God unto him? I have reserved to myself seven thousand men, who have not bowed the knee to the image of Baal. [5] Even so then at this present time also there is a remnant according to the election of grace. [6] And if by grace, then is it no more of works: otherwise grace is no more grace. But if it be of works, then is it no more grace: otherwise work is no more work. [7] What then? Israel hath not obtained that which he seeketh for; but the election hath obtained it, and the rest were blinded.

6. **Vs. 7 "What then? Israel failed to obtain what it was seeking. The elect obtained it, but the rest were hardened." (ESV) This is clearly referring to the history of the Jews. The "elect of Israel" obviously represents those of the Jews who believed or the Jewish remnant. The rest of the Jews were hardened or blinded at God's discretion. The apparent unfairness to these hardened is what Paul goes on to explain to the Gentile believers.**

[8] (According as it is written, God hath given them the spirit of slumber, eyes that they should not see, and ears that they should not hear;) unto this day. [9] And David saith, let their table be made a snare, and a trap, and a stumbling block, and a recompense unto them: [10] Let their eyes be darkened, that they may not see, and bow down their back always. [11] I say then, have they stumbled that they should fall? God forbid: but rather through their fall salvation is come unto the Gentiles, for to provoke them to jealousy.

7. **Vs. 11 "through their fall, salvation is come unto the Gentiles, for to provoke**

them to jealousy." (KJV) This is absolute proof that Paul is saying God used the fall of a portion of Israel to bring salvation to the Gentiles. And, God is using the faith of many Gentiles to make the hardened Jews jealous.

[12] Now if the fall of them be the riches of the world, and the diminishing of them the riches of the Gentiles; how much more their fullness? [13] For I speak to you Gentiles, inasmuch as I am the apostle of the Gentiles, I magnify mine office:

8. **Vs.13 "for I speak to you Gentiles inasmuch as I am the apostle of the Gentiles" (KJV) THIS IS IRREFUTABLE PROOF that Paul is speaking directly to the Gentiles, not Jews and Gentiles in this section of Romans.**

[14] If by any means I may provoke to emulation them which are my flesh, and might save some of them.15] For if the casting away of them be the reconciling of the world, what shall the receiving of them be, but life from the dead?[16] For if the firstfruit be holy, the lump is also holy: and if the root be holy, so are the branches.[17] And if some of the branches be broken off, and thou, being a wild

olive tree, wert grafted in among them, and with them partakest of the root and fatness of the olive tree;[18] Boast not against the branches. But if thou boast, thou bearest not the root, but the root thee. [19] Thou wilt say then, the branches were broken off, that I might be grafted in. [20] Well; because of unbelief they were broken off, and thou standest by faith. Be not high minded, but fear:[21] For if God spared not the natural branches, take heed lest he also spare not thee.[22] Behold therefore the goodness and severity of God: on them which fell, severity; but toward thee, goodness, if thou continue in his goodness: otherwise thou also shalt be cut off.[23] And they also, if they abide not still in unbelief, shall be grafted in: for God is able to graff them in again.[24] For if thou wert cut out of the olive tree which is wild by nature, and wert grafted contrary to nature into a good olive tree: how much more shall these, which be the natural branches, be grafted into their own olive tree?

9. **Vs. 24 "how much more shall these which be the natural branches be grafted into their own olive tree?" (KJV) Paul is distinguishing the Jews as the natural branches. This is added evidence that Paul is saying the distinction between**

Jews and Gentiles in terms of their heritage and God's plan is of major importance. He is using this clarification in an effort to reconcile their differences as believers in the church at Rome.

[25] For I would not, brethren, that ye should be ignorant of this mystery, lest ye should be wise in your own conceits; that blindness in part is happened to Israel, until the fulness of the Gentiles be come in.

10. **Vs. 25 "blindness in part is happened to Israel, until the fullness of the Gentiles be come in." (KJV) Paul is speaking directly to the Gentiles about what has happened to Israel and the future plan for Israel.**

[26] And so all Israel shall be saved: as it is written, there shall come out of Sion the Deliverer, and shall turn away ungodliness from Jacob: [27] For this is my covenant unto them, when I shall take away their sins. [28] As concerning the gospel, they are enemies for your sakes: but as touching the election, they are beloved for the fathers' sakes.

11. Vs. 28 "As regards the gospel, they are enemies for your sakes, but as regards election, they are beloved for the sake of their forefathers." (ESV) <u>Paul again uses the terminology of "election" to apply to the Jewish remnant</u>. THE "THEY" HAS TO BE THE JEWS, AND THE "YOUR SAKES" UNDENIABLY HAS TO REFER TO THE GENTILES.

[29] For the gifts and calling of God are without repentance.

12. Vs. 29 "For the gifts and calling of God are irrevocable." (ESV) The gifts and calling is of the Jewish believers who were defined in the previous verse as enemies for your sakes. Paul is saying that the promise to the Jewish remnant has not been revoked, retracted, or replaced! The Calvinists say the promises or covenant to the Jews is no longer in effect. They erroneously maintain that the Church is the "new Israel" taking the place of the Jewish remnant. This interpretation is in major conflict with Paul's writing in Chapter 11.

[30] For as ye in times past have not believed God, yet have now obtained mercy through their unbelief:[31] Even so have these also now not believed, that through your mercy they also may obtain mercy.[32] For God hath concluded them all in unbelief, that he might have mercy upon all.[33] O the depth of the riches both of the wisdom and knowledge of God! how unsearchable are his judgments, and his ways past finding out![34] For who hath known the mind of the Lord? or who hath been his counselor?[35] Or who hath first given to him, and it shall be recompensed unto him again?[36] For of him, and through him, and to him, are all things: to whom be glory forever. Amen.

Chapter 12

[1] I beseech you therefore, brethren, by the mercies of God, that ye present your bodies a living sacrifice, holy, acceptable unto God, which is your reasonable service.[2] And be not conformed to this world: but be ye transformed by the renewing of your mind, that ye may prove what is that good, and acceptable, and perfect, will of God.[3] For I say, through the grace given unto me, to every man that is among you, not to think of himself more highly than he ought to think; but to think soberly, according as

God hath dealt to every man the measure of faith.[4] For as we have many members in one body, and all members have not the same office:[5] So we, being many, are one body in Christ, and every one members one of another. [6] Having then gifts differing according to the grace that is given to us, whether prophecy, let us prophesy according to the proportion of faith; [7] Or ministry, let us wait on our ministering: or he that teacheth, on teaching; [8] Or he that exhorteth, on exhortation: he that giveth, let him do it with simplicity; he that ruleth, with diligence; he that sheweth mercy, with cheerfulness. [9] Let love be without dissimulation. Abhor that which is evil; cleave to that which is good. [10] Be kindly affectioned one to another with brotherly love; in honour preferring one another; [11] Not slothful in business; fervent in spirit; serving the Lord; [12] Rejoicing in hope; patient in tribulation; continuing instant in prayer; [13] Distributing to the necessity of saints; given to hospitality. [14] Bless them which persecute you: bless, and curse not.[15] Rejoice with them that do rejoice, and weep with them that weep.[16] Be of the same mind one toward another. Mind not high things, but condescend to men of low estate. Be not wise in your own conceits.

Chapter 13.

[1] Let every soul be subject unto the higher powers. For there is no power but of God: the powers that be are ordained of God. [2] Whosoever therefore resisteth the power, resisteth the ordinance of God: and they that resist shall receive to themselves damnation. [3] For rulers are not a terror to good works, but to the evil. Wilt thou then not be afraid of the power? do that which is good, and thou shalt have praise of the same: [4] For he is the minister of God to thee for good. But if thou do that which is evil, be afraid; for he beareth not the sword in vain: for he is the minister of God, a revenger to execute wrath upon him that doeth evil.[5] Wherefore ye must needs be subject, not only for wrath, but also for conscience sake.[6] For this cause pay ye tribute also: for they are God's ministers, attending continually upon this very thing.[7] Render therefore to all their dues: tribute to whom tribute is due; custom to whom custom; fear to whom fear; honour to whom honour. [8] Owe no man anything, but to love one another: for he that loveth another hath fulfilled the law.[9] For this, Thou shalt not commit adultery, Thou shalt not kill, Thou shalt not steal, Thou shalt not bear false witness, Thou shalt not covet; and if there be any other commandment, it is

briefly comprehended in this saying, namely, Thou shalt love thy neighbour as thyself.[10] Love worketh no ill to his neighbour: therefore love is the fulfilling of the law.[11] And that, knowing the time, that now it is high time to awake out of sleep: for now is our salvation nearer than when we believed.[12] The night is far spent, the day is at hand: let us therefore cast off the works of darkness, and let us put on the armor of light.[13] Let us walk honestly, as in the day; not in rioting and drunkenness, not in chambering and wantonness, not in strife and envying.[14] But put ye on the Lord Jesus Christ, and make not provision for the flesh, to fulfil the lusts thereof.

Chapter 14

[1] Him that is weak in the faith receive ye, but not to doubtful disputations. [2] For one believeth that he may eat all things: another, who is weak, eateth herb [3] Let not him that eateth despise him that eateth not; and let not him which eateth not judge him that eateth: for God hath received him [4] Who art thou that judgest another man's servant? to his own master he standeth or falleth. Yea, he shall be holden up: for God is able to make him stand. [5] One man

esteemeth one day above another: another esteemeth every day alike. Let every man be fully persuaded in his own mind [6] He that regardeth the day, regardeth it unto the Lord; and he that regardeth not the day, to the Lord he doth not regard it. He that eateth, eateth to the Lord, for he giveth God thanks; and he that eateth not, to the Lord he eateth not, and giveth God thanks.[7] For none of us liveth to himself, and no man dieth to himself.[8] For whether we live, we live unto the Lord; and whether we die, we die unto the Lord: whether we live therefore, or die, we are the Lord's.[9] For to this end Christ both died, and rose, and revived, that he might be Lord both of the dead and living.[10] But why dost thou judge thy brother? or why dost thou set at nought thy brother? for we shall all stand before the judgment seat of Christ.[11] For it is written, As I live, saith the Lord, every knee shall bow to me, and every tongue shall confess to God.[12] So then every one of us shall give account of himself to God.[13] Let us not therefore judge one another anymore: but judge this rather, that no man put a stumblingblock or an occasion to fall in his brother's way.

[14] I know, and am persuaded by the Lord Jesus, that there is nothing unclean of itself: but to him that esteemeth anything to be unclean, to him it is

unclean. [15] But if thy brother be grieved with thy meat, now walkest thou not charitably. Destroy not him with thy meat, for whom Christ died. [16] Let not then your good be evil spoken of: [17] For the kingdom of God is not meat and drink; but righteousness, and peace, and joy in the Holy Ghost. [18] For he that in these things serveth Christ is acceptable to God and approved of men.[19] Let us therefore follow after the things which make for peace, and things wherewith one may edify another.[20] For meat destroy not the work of God. All things indeed are pure; but it is evil for that man who eateth with offence. [21] It is good neither to eat flesh, nor to drink wine, nor any thing whereby thy brother stumbleth, or is offended, or is made weak. [22] Hast thou faith? have it to thyself before God. Happy is he that condemneth not himself in that thing which he alloweth. [23] And he that doubteth is damned if he eat, because he eateth not of faith: for whatsoever is not of faith is sin.

Chapter 15

[1] We then that are strong ought to bear the infirmities of the weak, and not to please

64

ourselves.[2] Let every one of us please his neighbour for his good to edification.[3] For even Christ pleased not himself; but, as it is written, The reproaches of them that reproached thee fell on me.[4] For whatsoever things were written aforetime were written for our learning, that we through patience and comfort of the scriptures might have hope.[5] Now the God of patience and consolation grant you to be likeminded one toward another according to Christ Jesus:[6] That ye may with one mind and one mouth glorify God, even the Father of our Lord Jesus Christ.[7] Wherefore receive ye one another, as Christ also received us to the glory of God. [8] Now I say that Jesus Christ was a minister of the circumcision for the truth of God, to confirm the promises made unto the fathers: [9] And that the Gentiles might glorify God for his mercy; as it is written, For this cause I will confess to thee among the Gentiles, and sing unto thy name.[10] And again he saith, Rejoice, ye Gentiles, with his people.[11] And again, Praise the Lord, all ye Gentiles; and laud him, all ye people.[12] And again, Esaias saith, There shall be a root of Jesse, and he that shall rise to reign over the Gentiles; in him shall the Gentiles trust.[13] Now the God of hope fill you with all joy and peace in believing, that ye may *abound in hope, through the power of the Holy Ghost.[14] And I myself also am persuaded of you, my brethren, that ye also are full of goodness, filled with all knowledge, able also to admonish one another. [15] Nevertheless, brethren, I have written the more boldly unto you in some sort, as putting you in mind, because of the grace that is given to me of God,[16] That I should be the minister of Jesus Christ to the Gentiles, ministering the gospel of God, that the offering up of the Gentiles might be acceptable, being sanctified by the Holy Ghost.*

13. Vs. 15-16 "...I have written more boldly...<u>putting you</u> in mind-...that I should be the minister of Jesus Christ to the Gentiles...that the offering up of <u>the Gentiles</u> might be acceptable" (KJV) Paul is addressing the Gentiles directly which again is added evidence that Paul is speaking to the Gentiles, not the Jews throughout Chapters 9-16.

[17] I have therefore whereof I may glory through Jesus Christ in those things which pertain to God.[18] For I will not dare to speak of any of those things which Christ hath not wrought by me, to make the Gentiles obedient, by word and deed,[19]

Through mighty signs and wonders, by the power of the Spirit of God; so that from Jerusalem, and round about unto Illyricum, I have fully preached the gospel of Christ.[20] Yea, so have I strived to preach the gospel, not where Christ was named, lest I should build upon another man's foundation: [21] But as it is written, To whom he was not spoken of, they shall see: and they that have not heard shall understand.[22] For which cause also I have been much hindered from coming to you.[23] But now having no more place in these parts, and having a great desire these many years to come unto you;[24] When so ever I take my journey into Spain, I will come to you: for I trust to see you in my journey, and to be brought on my way thitherward by you, if first I be somewhat filled with your company.[25] But now I go unto Jerusalem to minister unto the saints.[26] For it hath pleased them of Macedonia and Achaia to make a certain contribution for the poor saints which are at Jerusalem.[27] It hath pleased them verily; and their debtors they are. For if the Gentiles have been made partakers of their spiritual things, their duty is also to minister unto them in carnal things.[28] When therefore I have performed this, and have sealed to them this fruit, I will come by you into Spain.[29] And I am sure that, when I come unto you, I shall come in the fulness of the blessing of the gospel of Christ.[30] Now I beseech you, brethren, for the Lord Jesus Christ's sake, and for the love of the Spirit, that ye strive together with me in your prayers to God for me;[31] That I may be delivered from them that do not believe in Judaea; and that my service which I have for Jerusalem may be accepted of the saints;[32] That I may come unto you with joy by the will of God, and may with you be refreshed.[33] Now the God of peace be with you all. Amen.

Chapter 16

[1] I commend unto you Phebe our sister, which is a servant of the church which is at Cenchrea:[2] That ye receive her in the Lord, as becometh saints, and that ye assist her in whatsoever business she hath need of you: for she hath been a succourer of many, and of myself also.[3] Greet Priscilla and Aquila my helpers in Christ Jesus: [4] Who have for my life laid down their own necks: unto whom not only I give thanks, but also all the churches of the Gentiles. [5] Likewise greet the church that is in their house. Salute my well beloved Epaenetus, who is the

firstfruits of Achaia unto Christ. [6] Greet Mary, who bestowed much labour on us. [7] Salute Andronicus and Junia, my kinsmen, and my fellow prisoners, who are of note among the apostles, who also were in Christ before me. [8] Greet Amplias my beloved in the Lord. [9] Salute Urbane, our helper in Christ, and Stachys my beloved. [10] Salute Apelles approved in Christ. Salute them which are of Aristobulus' household. [11] Salute Herodion my kinsman. Greet them that be of the household of Narcissus, which are in the Lord. [12] Salute Tryphena and Tryphosa, who labour in the Lord. Salute the beloved Persis, which laboured much in the Lord. [13] Salute Rufus chosen in the Lord, and his mother and mine. [14] Salute Asyncritus, Phlegon, Hermas, Patrobas, Hermes, and the brethren which are with them. [15] Salute Philologus, and Julia, Nereus, and his sister, and Olympas, and all the saints which are with them. [16] Salute one another with a holy kiss. The churches of Christ salute you. [17] Now I beseech you, brethren, mark them which cause divisions and offences contrary to the doctrine which ye have learned; and avoid them. [18] For they that are such serve not our Lord Jesus Christ, but their own belly; and by good words and fair speeches deceive the hearts of the simple. [19] For your obedience is come abroad unto all men. I am glad therefore on your behalf: but yet I would have you wise unto that which is good, and simple concerning evil. [20] And the God of peace shall bruise Satan under your feet shortly. The grace of our Lord Jesus Christ be with you. Amen. [21] Timotheus my workfellow, and Lucius, and Jason, and Sosipater, my kinsmen, salute you. [22] I Tertius, who wrote this epistle, salute you in the Lord. [23] Gaius mine host, and of the whole church, saluteth you. Erastus the chamberlain of the city saluteth you, and Quartus a brother. [24] The grace of our Lord Jesus Christ be with you all. Amen.

[25] Now to him that is of power to stablish you according to my gospel, and the preaching of Jesus Christ, according to the revelation of the mystery, which was kept secret since the world began, [26] But now is made manifest, and by the scriptures of the prophets, according to the commandment of the everlasting God, made known to all nations for the obedience of faith: [27] To God only wise, be glory through Jesus Christ forever. Amen.

These additional 13 exhibits of internal evidence in Chapters of 9-16 make it abundantly clear that Paul is speaking

primarily to the Gentiles in this second part or last eight chapters of Romans.

The culmination of these 40 exhibits of internal evidence throughout the book of Romans substantiates that Two-Part Romans position is true!

Chapter V.

The Great Theological Implications

1. Calvinism is not a sufficient doctrine because the 2PR finding clarifies that Paul consistently declares that the elect are the chosen and foreknown people of God, the nation of Israel.

2. The Whosoever Will position is a sufficient doctrine and is supported by the 2PR finding and the harmony with all other Scripture with this finding. Salvation is for all who believe upon the Lord Jesus Christ.

3. The Calvinism doctrine is not sufficient because Paul boldly declares God has not revoked his

promises to Israel (Romans 11:28-29). Paul's stance is consistent with the promise plan presented throughout the Old Testament. One example of imperial evidence proving Two-Part Romans is found in Romans 7:1-5 as Paul clarifies "for I am speaking to those who know the law." Whenever Paul speaks of himself as a Jew, as well as other believing Jews, he and they are described as people of the promise—foreknown, chosen, and predestined. Paul explains that "God hath not cast away his people which he foreknew." (Romans 11:2) Paul says that Israel will eventually be grafted back because they are of the "natural branch." (Romans 11:24) The Jewish believers, by God's choice, were to be the first fruits. (Romans 11:15). Paul explains to the Gentiles they should not think God is unfair or unjust by choosing only a portion or the remnant of Israel who faithed God as the people of promise. That decision was God's prerogative just as "the potter determines the clay" (Romans 9:22). Paul clarifies that it was not the "children of the flesh" but "children of the promise" that were counted for the seed (Romans 9:8)..To choose only the faithful among the Israelites represented the "purpose of God according to election." (Romans 9:11)

The reminder of the Jews are described as receiving a partial hardening until the "fullness of the Gentiles has come in" (Romans 11:25b). "And in this way all Israel will be saved, as it is written" (Romans 11:26b). "As regards election, they are beloved for the sake of their forefathers for the gifts and the calling of God are irrevocable" (Romans 11:28b-29). Thus, Paul is conveying that the doctrines of foreknowledge, election, the chosen, the people of promise, and predestination are all valid doctrines of the Jewish remnant. The Jews who believe will be justified and glorified even though for some it will be at the end times by their faith and belief in Jesus Christ. Some will be saved before the end times because again the hardening is only partial.

To the Gentiles, Paul makes it clear that, as believers through faith, they have been grafted in as a branch and adopted as heirs. (Romans 11:17) Therefore, Paul declares there is now no condemnation for those that are not of the Jewish remnant. In fact, Paul goes to great extent to describe this <u>breakthrough as the mystery of the gospel that for the first time is revealed through his ministry</u>. Paul says, "This mystery is that the Gentiles are fellow heirs, members of the same body, and partakers of the promise in Christ Jesus through the gospel." (Ephesians 3:6)

This issue was the predominant issue of Paul's day: how could the Gentiles be saved or be reconciled to God since they were not of the promise? But, now as Paul says, the believing Gentiles are of the body, partakers and fellow heirs. The Gentiles who believe are described in Ephesians as once aliens of the promise to Israel (Ephesians 2:12), who were dead in their trespasses with no hope, but now they are believers who are alive in Christ. Whosoever will call upon the Lord shall be saved (Romans 10:13). Both groups of individuals, Jews and Gentiles, who have different heritages and history with God, now through faith are made one in Christ. This reconciliation between the Jewish and Gentile believers obviously represents the major purpose for Paul's writing to the church in Rome.

Paul refers to the choosing and calling of God in a different way when he refers to the Gentile believers such as in 1 Thessalonians 1:4 when he says, "loved of God, that he has chosen you because our gospel came to you not only in word, but also in power and in the Holy Spirit and with full conviction." It is in this spirit of conviction that Paul charges, "to walk in a manner worthy of God, who calls you into his kingdom and glory". This difference in calling involves the work of the Holy Spirit to convict. It does not indicate a choosing, election or predestination as a people of promise that Paul clearly states in reference to the Jewish remnant.

Yes, the foreknown, chosen, predestined Jews, the people of the promise, who have or will believe upon the Lord Jesus Christ shall be saved and are heaven bound! Yes, whosoever will, or all others who believe upon the Lord Jesus Christ shall be saved and are heaven bound! "Christ Jesus himself being the cornerstone in whom the whole structure, being joined together, grows into a holy temple in the Lord." (Ephesians 2:20b-21)

This wonderful breakthrough for the Gentiles is exactly what Luke describes in Acts 13:47-48, with Paul and Barnabas quoting Isaiah 49:6, "I have made you a light for the Gentiles, that you may bring salvation to the ends of the earth." When the Gentiles heard this, they were glad and honored the word of the Lord and all (or as many as) who were appointed (or many translations say ordained) to eternal life believed." (NIV) Many times this last verse is used as a proof text for Calvinism. However, the context describes a scene in which the Gentiles present had just heard for the first time they were included in God's plan! They were glad, indeed! Luke is making the point from a Jewish perspective that "all who were ordained" or all or as many of the Gentiles who had just understood their new appointed or ordained status believed. Note that Luke could have said, all who were chosen, elected, predestined, or foreknown, but obviously he did not say any of these.

He said instead that "all who were ordained" or now privileged, ranked, arranged, authorized (based on the Isaiah passage that had just been quoted) to receive salvation believed. In this setting, every last one of them believed! The good news is all the Gentiles are now appointed to be included in God's plan of salvation if they believe and have faith in Christ Jesus as their risen Savior.

The context of the Jewish-Gentile tension must always be taken into account. This ongoing clash and divide of that day is why Paul wrote Romans in such a way as to speak directly to each of these groups within the local church so they could understand even though they had far different heritages and were accustomed to different practices, they were to be united as one in Christ. Paul was obviously writing to reconcile the conflict between the Jewish and Gentile believers.

Chapter VI.

Harmony of 2PR with Other Scripture

Yes, the Two-Part Romans finding is in harmony with other Scripture concerning election! Ephesians, Galatians, and the Gospel of John also deal with election. Allow me to give you brief insights as to how verses in these books support the finding of Two-Part Romans. I have also included a brief survey of additional New Testament Scripture dealing with the elect. (KJV is quoted unless indicated otherwise)

EPHESIANS: In reading the Ephesians epistle, Paul clearly identifies himself in Chapter 1, "even as he chose us in him before the foundation of the world" (verse 4), "he predestined us for adoption as sons through Jesus Christ" (verse 5), "making known to us the mystery to his will" (verse 9). He adds in verse 12, "we were the first to hope in Christ". Paul is clearly speaking of himself and his fellow Jewish believers as the chosen people. This is in complete agreement with Deuteronomy 7:6 describing Israel as God's chosen people among all the people on the face of the earth.

Beginning at verse 13 of chapter 1, Paul says, "In him you also, when you heard the word of truth, the gospel of your salvation, and believed in him were sealed with the promised Holy Spirit." Paul begins Ephesians speaking about the wonderful heritage of Jewish believers as the elect chosen before the foundation of the world, but he says to the Gentiles, "when you heard....and believed, that was the gospel of your salvation." Paul is making a very important distinction which is consistent with the "Jews first" as the elect (remnant), and the Gentiles "when you believed" of Romans as well. The "we" as Paul speaks is clearly separate from the "you." This pronoun change cannot be denied.

The remainder of Ephesians beautifully describes how that Gentiles were "separated from Christ, alienated from the commonwealth of Israel and strangers to the covenants of promise having no hope" (2:12) "But, now in Christ Jesus you whom were once far off have been brought near by the blood of Christ" (2:13) The Jews were never strangers to the covenants, so Paul is absolutely and unequivocally speaking separate and directly to the Gentiles.

In Ephesians 3:4-6, Paul says that he is revealing the "mystery of Christ" and that it is "that the Gentiles are fellow heirs" and "partakers of promise in Christ Jesus through the gospel," So clearly, the Gentiles were not partakers of promise before.   Paul says in 3:8-9 that "...grace was given, to preach to the Gentiles" and "...bring light for everyone what is the plan of the mystery hidden for ages." (ESV) Paul would be so disappointed that we have confused the gospel saying things like the "elect" and "whosoever will" teachings are a paradox that cannot be explained and are deep mysteries beyond the finite minds of man.   Paul's explanation was to "bring light" not to mystify the precious gospel of Jesus Christ. All the confusion has been caused because so many have misinterpreted "the mystery of the gospel" for so long.

GALATIANS: Paul says of himself in 1:14, "when he who had set me apart before I was born and who called me by his grace" expressing his election as one of the Jewish remnant. Paul adds in 2:15, "we ourselves are Jews by birth and not Gentile sinners" so obviously there is a major and important difference in Paul's mind and teaching. In 3:15, "And the Scripture <u>foreseeing that God would justify the Gentiles by faith</u>, preached the gospel beforehand to Abraham saying, "In you shall all the nations be blessed". Obviously, the heritage of the Gentiles is quite different than "set me apart before I was born" as Paul says of himself as a Jew. This is exactly the same distinction that Paul made in Romans between the Jewish remnant (Chapters 1-8) and the Gentiles (Chapters 9-16).

Paul makes the same distinction in Galatians 4:4-6, "God sent forth his Son...to redeem those who were under the law (the Jews), so that we (the Jews) might receive adoption as sons. And because you (Gentiles), are sons, God has sent the Spirit of his Son into your hearts, (your hearts as Gentiles) crying "Abba! Father!" Note that when the believing Gentiles received the Holy Spirit, they too consciously knew they too belong to the Father. Paul continues the distinction throughout this letter that the "we" are the Jews and "you" are the Gentiles

Furthermore, in speaking directly to the Gentiles in 4:8-9, Paul says "Formerly, when you did not know God, you were enslaved to those that by nature are not gods. <u>But now</u> that you have come to know God, or rather <u>to be known by God</u>, how can you turn back again to the weak and elementary principles of the world?" Paul is clearly saying these Gentile believers were not known of God before, thus not of the Jewish elect for they were known of God before the foundation of the world. Paul is affirming the difference of the heritage of the Jewish elect (remnant) who had a faith relationship with God believing in the coming of Christ and the whosoever will of all nations, Gentiles. Both are saved by grace through faith in Jesus Christ.

Paul concludes this letter saying in 6:16, "And as for all (of the converted Gentiles) who walk by this rule, peace and mercy be upon them, <u>and upon the Israel of God.</u>" ESV This undeniable point of distinction is the same distinction that Paul maintained in Romans between Jewish believers of the remnant and Gentile believers. Various translations and scholars argue to remove the "and" or to translate it as explanative and not as a conjunction. In fact, this is the verse the Calvinist uses to argue that this verse implies a new Israel or a true Israel. But, the fact is that the term "new Israel" is not a term found in the New Testament at all. The position of a new Israel replacing the historic Israel relies on an external opinion of man and not the literal interpretations of God's word.

GOSPEL OF JOHN: In the gospel of John verse 1:11, John says, "He came to his own and his own people did not receive him" (Jews as his own people) "But, to all who did receive him, who believed in his name, he gave the right to become children of God" (verse 1:12). When one considers the context, John is saying that the portion of the Jews who did receive him (the remnant), he gave the right to become the children of God. This parallels the Two-Part Romans finding.

Having a clear understanding of the context of the gospel of John is so important. The Old Covenant was still in effect. The New Covenant, as we all know, took effect upon the death and resurrection of Christ. Obviously, the disciples and many others had believed in the coming of the Messiah and had a faith relationship with the Father before the death and resurrection of Christ. To overlook this context is to commit a major error.

Secondly, in terms of context, note that throughout this gospel Jesus is constantly dealing with issues and confrontations with the Jews, not the Gentiles. Jesus tells us in John 4:22 "for salvation is from the Jews". This substantiates what Paul said in Romans describing believing Jews as the first fruits. (Romans 8:23)

In John 3:14-15, the man who came unto Jesus by night, Nicodemus, a ruler of the Jews receives the answer, "And as Moses lifted up the serpent in the wilderness, so must the Son of Man be lifted up, that whoever believes in him may have eternal life." Furthermore, we all know the verse John 3:16 that follows also says, "whoever believes." Note that Jesus did not tell Nicodemus to confess with his mouth and believe in his heart. Instead, he said, "the Son of Man must be lifted up." In John 3:10, Jesus had admonished Nicodemus saying, " Art thou a master of Israel and know not these things?"

In John 6:36-37, Jesus said, "you have seen me and yet do not believe". The unbelieving Jews are those to whom Jesus is speaking because Jesus had just said in verse 32, "it was not Moses who gave you the bread of heaven?" Jesus is not speaking to the Gentiles as they did not receive the bread from heaven. Then, verse 37, "All that the Father gives me will come to me, and whoever comes to me I will never cast out." Jesus did not say those who believe, but those given. Then, Jesus added in verse 40, "For this is the will of my Father, that everyone who looks upon the Son and believes in him should have eternal life and I will raise him up on the last day." Thus, we have the "all that the Father gives me" and the "everyone who believes". The "all that the Father gives me" parallels the elect remnant as described in Romans chapters 1-8 and the "everyone who believes" parallels the "whosoever believes" of Romans chapters 9-16.

The "all that the Father gives me" are the saints living in the presence of Christ! They already had a faith relationship with God, believing in God's promise of a coming Messiah. Remember, Jesus had said, "I must be lifted up." The new covenant was still to come. These old covenant saints living in the presence of Jesus were the ones Jesus describes as given to him by the Father. Jesus knew them because He and the Father are one. Because they had already believed, Jesus knew them from the beginning of His ministry on earth.

In verse 6:44, "no one can come to me unless the Father who sent me draws him" is followed in verse

45 by the direct quote of Isaiah 54:13, when Isaiah says to the Jews "all your children will be taught by God. Everyone who has heard and learned from the Father comes to me." This context requires us to interpret verse 44 as applying to the Jewish remnant.

This finding is consistent with 6:64-66, "some of you do not believe... for Jesus knew from the beginning who those were and ... who it was who would betray him" (ESV). "And he said, this is why I told you that no one can come to me unless it is granted him by the Father." (ESV) Jesus is saying those who had believed in God and his promise of a Messiah knew God and God knew them. These who already had a faith relationship with the Father like all the Old Testament saints were granted or given to Jesus by the Father. "After this many of his disciples turned back and no longer walked with him" (ESV). In this context, he is speaking to the Jews, knowing that only some had already believed in the Father. This remnant "was granted him by the Father."

In confronting the nonbelieving Jews, Jesus tells them in 8:44, "You are of your father the devil, and your will is to do your father's desires. He was a murderer from the beginning." And in 8:47 Jesus said, "Whosoever is of God hears the words of God.

The reason you (the unbelieving Jews) do not hear them is that you are not of God." This is dealing with those Jews who had not previously believed. This passage has nothing to do with the Gentiles.

Jesus says in 9:39, "For judgment I came into the world that those who do not see (Gentiles) may see, and those who see (the Jews who have yet to believe) may become blind." This is exactly what Paul says in Romans 11:25, "that blindness in part is happened to Israel until the fullness of the Gentiles has come in."

We can see this application even clearer in John 10:14 and 16, "I am the good shepherd. I know my own (remnant Jews) and my own know me." And, Jesus says, "I have other sheep (those who will believe in the future) that are not of this fold. (not of the remnant) I must bring them also, and they will listen to my voice. So, there will be one flock, one shepherd." The one flock will be the believing Jews and the believing Gentiles.

In John 12:32 Jesus says, "And I, when I am lifted up from the earth, will draw all people to myself". Jesus said earlier that only those given to him by the Father or "unless the Father who sent me draws them." Now Jesus is saying there will be a big change when he is lifted up (on the cross). No longer will it be the ones sent and the ones given as noted in the previous chapters, but it will also be those drawn to myself. This difference is further emphasized when Jesus says in 16:7-8, "I tell you the truth: it is to your advantage that I go away, for if I do not go away, the Helper (Holy Spirit) will not come to you. But if I go, I will send him to you. And when he comes, he will convict the world concerning sin and righteousness and judgment." Yes, the Holy Spirit will convict the whole world, the Gentiles or all nations, not just the Jewish remnant, but only when he (Holy Spirit) comes.

As Jesus expresses his prayer of 17:9, he says to the Father, "I am praying for those you have given me, for they are yours." (those who believed in the coming of Christ and had a faith relationship with the Father before the resurrection) Verse 17:12 continues the prayer for those "not one of them has been lost except the son of destruction, that the Scripture might be fulfilled." Again, Jesus speaks of those given (including the disciples as part of the elect remnant) and the one Judas who was lost. Those "given" are different than those described "when I am lifted up, I will draw all people to myself." This parallels the finding of Two-Part Romans.

In conclusion, Jesus prayed in 17: 18-20, "As you sent me into the world, so I have sent them (the disciples) into the world. And for their sake I consecrate myself, that they also may be sanctified in truth. <u>I do not ask for these only, but also for those who will believe</u> in me through their word that they may be <u>all in one.</u>" The mystery of the gospel is revealed as the way, the truth, and the life for "those who will believe," the Jew first and now the Gentiles!

<u>There should be no conflict and confusion in the gospel. There is a only a difference in the heritage of the elect, the Jewish remnant who believed, and all others who believe.</u>   Paul went to great extents to teach this truth. <u>Now we are one, "built on the foundation of the apostles and prophets, Christ Jesus himself being the cornerstone, in whom the whole structure, being joined together grows into a holy temple in the Lord</u>." (Ephesians 2:21)

Other New Testament Scriptures which affirm that the Jewish remnant represents the elect include:

(1) Thessalonians: When Paul addresses the Thessalonians in his first letter he says, "Knowing brethren beloved, <u>of your election of God for our gospel came not unto in word only, but also in power, and in the Holy Ghost, and in much assurance...</u> (1:4-

5 ESV)." These verses affirm that God includes these new converts because their salvation was by conviction and faith on their part after hearing the Gospel. In 1:9, the new converts are commended because they "turned to God from idols." (ESV) In his second letter to the Thessalonian church, Paul says, "we are bound to give thanks always to God for you...because God had from the beginning chosen you to salvation through sanctification of the Spirit and belief of the truth (2:13)." Paul is affirming that these converts received salvation as result of sanctification of the Spirit and their belief of the truth and that this was God's plan from the beginning. Paul had said earlier in the same chapter 2, verse 10, "in them that perish; because they received not the love of the truth, that they might be saved." The distinction is very clear that these converts were not predestined before the foundation of the world as were the Jewish remnant who had believed in God and the promise of the coming of a Messiah. Their (Gentiles) way of salvation under the New Covenant which God had determined, decided or chose from the beginning. It involved their individual response to the conviction and sanctification by the Holy Spirit. They received the love of the truth and they turned from the idols. Paul reiterates this position when says if they "choose

<u>not to receive</u> the love of the truth, they were not saved (2:10)."

(2) Jude: The writing of Jude sometimes is used to uphold Calvinism but it actually affirms the Jewish remnant as the as God's elect people. Jude was the brother of James, the head of the Jerusalem church. This evidence identifies this Jude as the half-brother of Jesus. In Jude verses 3, 7, and 20, it is clear that Jude had a longstanding relationship with the recipients. This context combined with the many references to the Old Testament clearly substantiates that the recipients were Jewish. Thus, when Jude says in verse 2, "to those who are called, beloved in God the Father and kept for Jesus Christ", this "keeping" is consistent with the doctrine of the elect remnant of Jews as we described earlier in the Two-Part Romans (2PR) discussion. Jude concludes his letter saying "Now to him who is able to keep you from stumbling and to present you blameless before the presence of his glory with great joy. (ESV)" This "keep you" again is consistent with the elect being the Jewish remnant.

(3) Hebrews 2:13 also is used from time to time as a Calvinist proof text. One must remember that the letter to the Hebrews is a letter to the Jewish

Christians because the term Hebrew is first used in Scripture to refer to Abraham (Genesis 14:13, 40:15) and his descendants. Therefore, when the writer says in 2:13, "...behold, I and the children which God hath given me", he is citing Isaiah 8:18 which is also quoted by Jesus in John 17:2. As explained earlier in referencing the Gospel of John, the "children given" aligns with elect people of Israel who believed or the Jewish remnant. The verse of Hebrews 2:13 is not referring to Gentile believers.

(4) 1 Peter 1:1-2 is yet another favorite reference of the Calvinist. Just as Paul was the acclaimed apostle to the Gentiles, Peter was the apostle to the Jews (Galatians 2:8). Peter clearly describes his recipients in verse 1 "to those who reside as aliens scattered throughout Pontus, Galatia, Cappadocia, Asia and Bithynia who are chosen according to the foreknowledge of God the Father... (NAS)." The word scattered is the Greek word "diaspora" which means dispersion. In the New Testament, it refers to dispersing of the Jews throughout the world such as used also in John 7:35 and in James 1:1. Peter, the apostle to the Jews is writing to his Jewish brethren who were very familiar with the Old Testament. In the Old Testament, the people of Israel are described as the called-out ones, chosen, or the elect.

(Deuteronomy 7:6, 14:2; Psalms 105:43, 135:4)
Therefore, this passage of 1 Peter 1:1-2 further affirms
that the elect are indeed the believers of the people of
Israel who represent the Jewish remnant.

(5) The passages concerning the last days of the
tribulation such as Matthew 24:22, 31; Luke 18:7
Revelation 13:8, 17:8 speak of the elect who cry to him
and for their sake, the days will be cut short. This is
even more evidence that those of the Jewish remnant
are the elect because the church has already been
taken up in the rapture. (1 Thessalonians 4:17)

(6) Revelation: All agree that John wrote this epistle
from the isle of Patmos and that the seven churches
as described in 1:11 were located in Asia within a 250-
mile radius of the Isle of Patmos. As to who are the
recipients of this writing is very significant. The
evidence that John was writing to the Jews in
tribulation is provided in 2:9," I know thy works, and
tribulation...and I know the blasphemy of those which
say they are Jews and are not"; and in 3:9, which say
they are Jews and, are not...". Obviously, this
revelation to John emphasizes the significance as to
whether the recipients were truly Jews. Paul had
clarified in Galatians 2:9 that James, Peter and John
had agreed that Paul should go to the Gentiles and

they go to the circumcised or Jews. Historically, John the revelator has always been considered to be an apostle to the Jews. So, John sharing this revelation primarily with the Jews is as expected. This context cannot be denied.

In 2:26, the text reads, "And he that overcometh and keepeth my works unto the end, to him will I give the power over the nations". This term nations in the original Greek language is the word "ethnon" and can be translated either nations or Gentiles. Throughout the New Testament in verses such as Matthew 4:15,10:5,20:25, Luke 22:25, Acts 9:15,13:47,14:2, Romans 3:29,9:24,15:12 Galatians 2:15, Ephesians 3:1, 1 Timothy 2:7; 1 Peter 4:3, this same word is translated Gentiles. When this word is translated Gentiles in Revelation 2:26, the evidence is mounting and clear that the revelation to John is very intentionally speaking to the Jews who overcometh and will have power over the nations or Gentiles in these end times. This is in perfect harmony with Isaiah 11:11-12:6; Ezekiel 11:14-18 and 37:1-18; as well as Jeremiah 15:14-15.

In Revelation 7:4-8, the Scripture is very clear that the 144,000 were from the tribes of Israel as the twelve tribes are specifically listed. Gentile believers are not referred to at all.

Additional evidence that the revelation is primarily speaking to the Jews include: (a) the entire book refers to symbols and elements of the heritage of Israel and worship within the Jewish temple (b) the deliverance of those who overcome mirrors the deliverance of Israel from their bondage in Egypt (c) the book was not written in the distinct style of the Greek language of that day indicating that it was originally written in Hebrew and later translated into Greek.

This finding is consistent with the writing of Paul as he describes the rapture of the Church before the end times in 1 Thessalonians 4:16b-17: "the dead in Christ shall rise first: Then we which are alive and remain shall be caught up together with them in the clouds, to meet the Lord in the air." The revelation of John is primarily a plea to the Jews.

John's writing in Revelation also makes a distinction between the book of life (Revelation 3:5, 17:8, 20:12, 20:15) and the Lamb's book of life (Revelation 13:8 and Revelation 20:15). John indicates in Revelation 20:12 that some of the names in the book of life are blotted out. This blotting out is also described in

Psalm 69:28. Those that were or will be blotted out represent the Jews who failed or will fail to believe.

Why do we have this distinction? The context of John writing to the Jews indicates that this all-important distinction is referring to those of the elect Jews whose names were written in the book of life before the foundation of the world who believed or not believed. As described in Revelation, these Jews are saved through faith in Christ in the last days in contrast to all of the Gentiles and Jews of the Church who were saved earlier. Those who were saved earlier (before these last days) represent those of the Church who are raptured before the time of the Great Tribulation. This is in perfect agreement with Paul's description of two olive branches with the natural branch (the remnant of the Jews who believe) being restored in the end. (Romans 11:23-24)

Again, the Two-Part Romans (2PR) finding substantiates a consistency in the interpretation of all Scripture. Consistency and congruency or harmony of Scripture trumps any and all theories about Scripture. "Jesus Christ is the same yesterday, and today and forever "Hebrews 13:8 (NIV). "For I the Lord do not change" Malachi 3:6 (ESV). "I am the Alpha and the Omega" says the Lord God, "the One

who is, who was, and who is coming, the Almighty."
Revelation 1:8 (HCSB).

This interpretation of Revelation upholds the finding
of Two-Part Romans. (2PR) In terms of Calvinism,
John Calvin omitted the book of Revelation from his
New Testament Commentary. Martin Luther wrote in
his Preface to the Revelation of St. John in 1522, "...I
consider it to be neither apostolic or prophetic. I can
in no way detect that the Holy Spirit produced it."
And, the Calvinist Zwingli said of Revelation, "it is not
a book of the Bible." (Crutchfield, *Revelation in the
New Testament,* 34)

In summary, God Word is inerrant and consistent
being of one author! The Jewish remnant or believers
of the elect nation of Israel were described as the elect
throughout the Old Testament and continue to be
described as the elect in the New Testament. God
remains true and faithful to his promises.

Chapter VII.

Theological Viewpoint

In terms of theological views, one must keep in mind that the classical covenant or reformed theological position was not formulated until the early 1600's and that the classical dispensational view originated in the early 1800's. Other variations of these views (such as the renewal covenant or progressive dispensational views) have emerged in more recent years but all of these viewpoints or systems of thought for the most part hinge on one issue: the relationship between Israel and the Church. Either the promises or covenant to Israel have been replaced or postponed to some degree dependent upon the variation of viewpoint.

This finding of Two-Part Romans (2PR) resolves that there is a consistent fulfillment of all God's promises and all prophesies. This finding confirms that the elect that Paul describes in Romans corresponds to the people of the Jewish remnant described in the Old Testament as the elect. As stated in the Old Testament, Israel was to be the light unto all nations or all people. (Isa. 42:6, 49:6) Even through a portion of the Israel is blinded or hardened for a season, there is portion not blinded or harden who continue to be God's chosen people and God's chosen instruments to bring the light to all people who will believe, saved by grace through faith. The elect (Jewish remnant) were saved in the same fashion, by grace through faith. As being the people of God's chosen nation of Israel, Jesus knew them before the foundation of the world (the elect or the Jewish remnant including Paul). They were and even now, as the remnant continue to represent the foreknown and predestined elect. God has purposed them as agents of redemption for whosoever will believe. When Jesus died on the cross, the kingdom's survival was not dependent upon people responding to the gospel message. This is because the elect (who were the Jewish remnant of believers) remained. They were God's people on earth. God knew them because they had a faith relationship with God prior to the ministry of Jesus on earth. This was just as God told Elijah in 1 Kings 19:18, "I have reserved for myself 7,000 of Israel who have not bowed to the knee to Baal." Paul quotes this also in Romans 11:4 and then adds in 11:5, "so too, at the present time there is a remnant chosen by grace."

This consistent fulfillment position matches up beautifully with the parables of Jesus in that: (a) many are called (whosoever will believe who are drawn through the convicting Holy Spirit once Jesus is lifted up), but few are chosen (the Jewish remnant who were of the predestined people of Israel and represented only the portion that had believed) (b) the continued great growth of the singular mustard seed (c) the importance of the continued sewing of seed and that some the seed will take root (d) the importance of the continued and concerted focus upon the lost sheep, coin and son that they might be saved. Jesus emphatically stated he did not come to destroy the Law or the Prophets but to fulfill them. (Mt. 5:17) Jesus clearly stated that salvation is from the Jews. (John 4:22) This scriptural evidence supports continued and consistent fulfillment, not a replacement or redefinition of Israel. Again, God's plan has always been and continues to be the use the

Jewish elect as his agents of redemption to bring light to all people. This is true even to the extent that Israel might be made jealous --"rather through their trespass salvation has come to the Gentiles, so as to make Israel jealous" (Rom. 11:11). Paul affirms that someday the full inclusion of Israel will involve even greater riches (Romans 11:12).

The *Promise Plan of God* theological view as presented by Walter C. Kaiser Jr. is much aligned with this consistent fulfillment finding even though he does not state that Paul wrote Romans in two-parts.

In the final analysis, this consistent fulfillment position underscores even more the inerrancy of God's Word. God's Word is in fact without error and without contradiction. It is of one author. It is consistent. It is congruent. The finding of Two-Part Romans upholds these truths.

This consistent fulfillment position upholds a position of the greater grace, the greater sovereignty, and the greater inerrancy when compared with the Calvinistic and Reformed theology systems.

All God's Word and all prophecy in God's Word counts!

"For verily I say unto you, till heaven and earth pass, one jot or one little tittle shall in no wise pass from the law, till all shall be fulfilled" (Matthew 5:18 *KJV).*

Chapter VIII.

Why Many Baptists Became Fullerite Calvinists

This writing continues to present objective evidence so you can arrive at a fully informed conclusion with great confidence. In this chapter, the evidence referenced involves historical accounts and actual writings of the principal leaders involved. (The underlined is mine for emphasis.)

The following documented historical accounts and actual writings provide conclusive evidence that:

1. Andrew Fuller realized that the high or hyper-Calvinism of John Gill was wrong and searched for an answer.

2. Andrew Fuller developed a theological system that was profoundly influenced by the writings of Jonathan Edwards.

3. Jonathan Edwards was an accomplished philosopher and used philosophical or human reasoning in his finding that all people have a responsibility to respond to the gospel, even though, as he expressed, "They may have a kind of religious love, and yet have no saving grace." This quote is from his writing of *Religious Affections*.

4. Many Baptists became followers of Fuller's brand of Calvinism because his position agreed with Scripture that the gospel should be offered to all people but maintained the five points of Calvinism.

5. Andrew Fuller maintained that all people have a duty to respond to the gospel, but that of all

those responding, only those of the predestined elect will truly be saved.

Exhibit A. Historian David Benedict in his writing *Fifty Years Among the Baptist* (1860) describes how Gillites and Fullerites of England in the 1800s were at great odds over the doctrine of Calvinism per this excerpt.

"[L]arge bodies of Baptists were in a state of ferment and agitation, in consequence of some modifications of their old Calvinistic creed, as displayed in the writings of Andrew Fuller of Kettering, England. This famous man maintained that the atonement of Christ was general in its nature, but particular in its application, in opposition to our old divines, who held that Christ died for the elect only. He also made the distinction between the natural and moral inability of men."

"Dr. John Gill of London was, in his day, one of the most distinguished divines among the English Baptists, and as he was a noted advocate for the old system of a limited atonement, the terms "Gillites" and "Fullerites" were often applied to the parties in the discussion. Those who espoused the views of Mr. Fuller were denominated Armenians by the Gillite men, while they, in their turn styled their opponents hyper-Calvinists. Both parties claimed to be orthodox and evangelical, and differed but little on any other points except those which have been named."

Exhibit B. Andrew Fuller struggled in his own conversion experience with the doctrines of high or Hyper-Calvinism. This excerpt is from "Andrew Fuller" by Phil Roberts, Chapter 3 in the book, *Theologians of the Baptist Tradition*, editors Timothy George and David S. Dockery, 2001.

"Andrew Fuller was reared in a high Calvinistic context. He wrote that as a youth the preaching of his pastor was 'not adapted to awaken my conscience and seldom did he say anything to unbelievers.' Consequently, his conversion was a protracted, troubled affair and mirrored the questions he would later forcefully address: May one apply directly to Christ for salvation without any certainty that he or she is elect? Should everyone be exhorted to believe in Christ?"

Exhibit C. Andrew Fuller, as stated in his own writings, was greatly influenced by the writings of Jonathan Edwards. The following is an excerpt from the article written by Obbie Todd on the website *Jonathan Edwards Studies* entitled, "Did Jonathan Edwards Inspire the Modern Missionary Movement?"

April 2016.

"It is important to remember that while the two men lived in the same enlightened century, they also occupied both poles of it. Andrew Fuller was born in Soham, England in 1754: the year that Edwards' *Freedom of the Will* was published and four years before Edwards' death. Thus, to say that the Congregationalist and the Particular Baptist were contemporaries would be false. However, their historical proximity was beneficial for Fuller, as he faced the same eighteenth-century rationalism as his predecessor. Edwards indeed lived on in his writings, serving to fuel Fuller's theological aims years after his death. (Edwards' *Freedom of the Will* was recommended to him by Robert Hall of Arnsby in 1775.) Fuller responded forcefully to those who questioned his allegiance to Edwards: "*We have some who have been giving out, of late, that 'If Sutcliff and some others had preached more of Christ, and less of Jonathan Edwards, they would have been more useful.' If those who talked thus preached Christ half as much as Jonathan Edwards did, and were half as useful as he was, their usefulness would be double what it is.*"

Edwards' *Freedom of the Will* helped him reconcile

evangelistic preaching with the divine sovereignty of Calvinism. In his second edition of *The Gospel Worthy of All Acceptation* (1801), Fuller acknowledges his debts to Edwards' *Freedom of the Will* in distinguishing between natural and moral inability. In addition, Edwards *Religious Affections* not only aided Fuller in his response to the high Calvinism of John Gill and John Brine, but has equipped Fuller to refute Sandemanianism ("easy-believism") as espoused by Archibald McLean. Fuller boasted that Edwards' sermons on justification gave him *"more satisfaction on that important doctrine than <u>any human performance</u> which I have read."*

Exhibit D: Jonathan Edwards was a philosopher as well as a theologian. The following is an excerpt from *Biography*, Edwards Center, Yale University, Marsden 2003, p. 66.

"Jonathan Edwards entered Yale College in 1716, at just under the age of 13. In the following year, he became acquainted with John Locke's *An Essay Concerning Human Understanding*, which influenced him profoundly. During his college studies, he kept notebooks labeled "The Mind,"

"Natural Science" (containing a discussion of the atomic theory), "The Scriptures," and "Miscellanies." He had a grand plan for a work on natural and mental philosophy, and drew up for himself rules for its composition."

Exhibit E. Jonathan Edwards, as a college student, regarded the election of some to salvation and of others to eternal damnation as a horrible doctrine. This excerpt is from *Biography*, Edwards Center Yale University, Marsden 2003, p. 51.

"The years 1720 to 1726 are partially recorded in the diary of Jonathan Edwards and in the resolutions for his own conduct which he drew up at this time. He had long been an eager seeker after salvation and was not fully satisfied as to his own conversion until an experience in his last year in college, when he lost his feeling that the election of some to salvation and of others to eternal damnation was "a horrible doctrine," and reckoned it "exceedingly pleasant, bright and sweet." He now took a great and new joy in taking in the beauties of nature, and delighted in the allegorical interpretation of the Song of Solomon."

Exhibit F. In 1754, Jonathan Edwards primarily used a philosophical argument in the writing "On the Freedom of the Will," as confirmed below in excerpts from that writing.

"Mr. Locke says, 'The Will is perfectly distinguished from desire; which in the very same action may have quite contrary tendency from that which our wills sets us upon. A man, says he, whom I cannot deny, may oblige me to use persuasions to another, which, at the same time I am speaking, I may wish not prevail.'"

"It appears from what has been said, that these terms necessary, impossible, are often used by philosophers and metaphysicians in a sense quite diverse from their common and original signification; for they apply them to many cases in which no opposition is supposable."

"The subject and predicate of a proposition, which affirms existence of something, may have a full, fixed, and certain connection several ways."

"It is agreeable to common sense, and the natural notions of mankind, to suppose moral necessity to be consistent with praise and blame, reward, and punishment."

Exhibit G. Jonathan Edwards in his writing *Religious Affections* **reasoned that expression of religious affections does not mean one is saved. The following are excerpts from that writing.**

"The holy Scriptures do everywhere place religion very much in the affection; such as fear, hope, love, hatred, desire, joy, sorrow, gratitude, compassion, and zeal."

"It is no evidence that religious affections are saving, or that they are otherwise, that there is an appearance of love in them."

"But with respect to love; it is plain by the Scripture, that persons may have a kind of religious love, and yet have no saving grace."

Exhibit F. Andrew Fuller wrote *The Gospel Worthy of All Acceptation,* **in which he expresses it is the duty of all men to respond to the gospel even though he believes not all men are predestined to be saved. The following are excerpts from that writing per the 1801 edition.**

"First, there is no dispute about the doctrine of election, or any of the discriminating doctrines of grace. They are allowed on both sides; and it is granted that none ever did or ever will believe in Christ, but those who are chosen of God from eternity." (Preface)

"Fuller found much satisfaction in this distinction; as it appeared to him to carry with it its own evidence—to be clearly and fully contained in the Scriptures—and calculated to disburden the Calvinistic system of a number of calumnies with which its enemies have loaded." (Preface)

"The question is not whether unconverted sinners be the subjects of exhortation, but whether they ought to be exhorted to perform spiritual duties. It is beyond all dispute that the Scriptures do exhort them to many things." (Preface)

"Christ and his apostles, without any hesitation, called on sinners to 'repent and believe the gospel'; but we, considering them as poor, impotent, and depraved creatures, have been disposed to drop this part of the Christian ministry."

"Neither Augustine nor Calvin, who each in his day defended predestination, and the other doctrines connected with it, ever appear to have thought of denying it to be the duty of every sinner who has heard the gospel to repent and believe in Jesus Christ."

"I believe it is the duty of every minister of Christ plainly and faithfully to preach the gospel to all who will hear it: and as I believe the inability of men to do spiritually good things to be wholly of the moral and therefore of the criminal kind and that it is their duty to love the Lord Jesus Christ and trust in Him for salvation, though they do not..."

Concluding Points:

1. Both Jonathan Edwards and Andrew Fuller struggled with their own salvation and the doctrine of high Calvinism early in their lives.

2. Jonathan Edwards was an accomplished philosopher and used philosophy to explain his belief that many could believe by human will but not be saved.

3. Andrew Fuller accepted the rationale of Edwards as a solution to the "calumnies" against Calvinism.

4. Andrew Fuller advocated that it is the duty of all men to believe even though he believed of all those responding or believing, only the predestined elect would be saved. Fuller maintained that the atonement of Christ is general in nature but particular in application.

5. Many Baptists continue to agree with Fullerite Calvinism. History shows that this "Fuller Fix" or Fuller's newfound system was greatly influenced by Jonathan Edwards, who used human philosophy to reconcile the scriptural contradictions of Calvinism. This new system was derived from new human reasoning and not new insights involving God's revelation.

"Beware lest any man spoil you through philosophy and vain deceit, after the tradition of men, after the rudiments of the world, and not after Christ" Colossians 2:8 (KJV).

Chapter IX.

Points of Summation

Your decision to affirm the finding of Two-Part Romans is of upmost importance. As a "member of the jury", you have been presented abounding evidence to support this finding which resolves the puzzle concerning Calvinism and Whosoever Will. The following points affirm this conclusion.

1. God's Word is consistent. As the inspired and inerrant Word of God, there is only one author of Scripture and therefore whenever there is a question of interpretation, one must find in favor of the most scripture interpreted within its context which is most consistent. This finding provides a consistent interpretation

and harmony of all Scripture. All the prophecies fall neatly into place. This finding upholds the doctrines of predestination and election as well as the doctrine of whosoever will. There is no conflict. This is not a two-track salvation in that Jews and Gentiles alike are saved through faith. There is no need to redefine, replace, or retract God's promise to Israel or to invent a "new Israel" or to deny the eventual restoration of Israel as Scripture abundantly upholds. God's Word is consistent and congruent.

In comparison, the Calvinistic viewpoint is dependent upon a systematic theological approach based on "proof text". Secondly, the Calvinistic viewpoint stands in direct conflict with major portions of Scripture thus creating, as the Calvinists say, "a mystery that cannot be explained to the finite minds of men."

2. <u>God is faithful to his promises</u>. The Word of God clearly reveals that the Jews are to be the channel of salvation to the Gentiles or all nations. (Isaiah 42:6 and 49:6, Luke 2:32, Acts 13:47) As stated by Paul in Romans, the

Gentiles did not replace the Jewish remnant. Paul declares that the natural olive branch will be revived and God's promises will not be revoked. Romans 11:28-29 cannot be discarded. God expanded salvation for all men through His special relationship with the Jewish remnant throughout the ages.

3. <u>Man is fallible</u>. God's Holy Word is not. Great men of God throughout the last 2,000 years have made invaluable contributions, but they were and are human. They made mistakes. As history reveals, and most of us have witnessed, many great scholars have changed their interpretation of a particular passages of Scripture within their own lifetime. Opinions of the past are just that.

For more than 500 years, history documents a great debate and conflict over an essential doctrine of God's Word: the salvation of man. Obviously, one or more of the teachings is very wrong and has been for a long time. Does anyone even suggest that it is God's will for the believers of His Church to have this great conflict and divide concerning this most essential doctrine?

4. <u>God's word reveals and does not conceal the way of salvation.</u> This finding is very consistent with what the Apostle Paul says in scripture concerning the mystery of the Gospel revealed beginning with his ministry. Many maintain that the Gospel is far too mysterious to be understood by the finite minds of men, and they claim the conflict of whosoever will and predestination is meant to be a great mystery claiming Deuteronomy 29:29 of the Old Testament as the proof. Such a conclusion is very contrary to Paul's writings in the New Testament as he consistently strives to reveal and explain, not to confound and confuse. Man is the author of confusion, not God.

If you feel it is better to: (1) build a doctrine upon selected proof texts which are in conflict with major portions of God's Word, and; (2) believe God breaks his promises even when Paul said explicitly in Scripture that God does not, and; (3) uphold a doctrine formulated by men 500 years after the New Testament times which was new and has been a point of major conflict among scholars ever since its inception, and; (4) feel it was Paul's intention to conceal the mystery rather than reveal the mystery as he explicitly stated in his letters, then Calvinism is the doctrine for you.

Otherwise, based upon the abounding evidence as stated herein, you must find that Two-Part Romans is truth. And, that the Calvinism is not a sufficient doctrine. The puzzle or conflict between Calvinism and the whosoever will position is resolved with the finding of Two-Part Romans (2PR).

I conclude with the prayer as that of Apostle Paul, that "This is good and acceptable in the sight of God our Savior, who desires all people to be saved." (1 Tim 2:3-4 KJV)

ABOUT THE AUTHOR

Dr. Brent Lay, D.Min., is a graduate of Union University (Tennessee), University of Memphis, Southern Baptist Theological Seminary (Kentucky), and Trinity Theological Seminary (Indiana). His 30-plus years of vocational ministry includes serving as a headmaster of a Christian school, a director of missions, a minister of education and outreach, and as the Associate Pastor at Englewood Baptist Church where he preached in the early worship service for seven years. During his tenure of twenty-five years on the staff at Englewood, the church more than tripled in attendance as well as the number of annual baptisms.

He is also the founder and development director for the *Million More by 34'* national campaign aimed at Southern Baptists baptizing a million more each year beginning in 2034. This strategy deploys part time connection coordinators or church missionaries similar in dynamics to the highly successful Apartment Life Coordinator ministry which has expanded exponentially to more than 25 states in recent years. More information about this church missionary initiative can be found at millionmoreby34.com.

Join the Movement!

Million More by 34'

To enable, equip, and empower 200,000 bi-vocational connection coordinators or church missionaries **by year 2034,** who each will reach at least 5 family units per year resulting in at least 5 baptisms each for a total of a **million more baptisms per year**.

This approach represents the most doable, effective and efficient mission strategy for churches of any size!

Find details at millionmoreby34.com and in the book, *The Passion Driven Church*.

(to be released by March 2024)

Additional copies of this book can be

purchased through Amazon Books.

Church Missionary Description on the next page

Church Missionary

Highly trained person called by God,

connected to the local church, to

cross cultural barriers for the cause

of the Gospel of Jesus Christ

- **Based on 34 years of proven success with 30 part-time people serving in 6 different churches**

- **Highest and best use of volunteers**

- **Superior discipleship in that the person who reaches is also the person who initially teaches and disciples**

- **Easy for any size church to adopt this strategy without making major changes**

- **Multiplies the outreach efforts of the Pastor**

- **Provides a great approach in dealing with the "new normal"**

See website at: churchmissionarymovement.com

Made in United States
Orlando, FL
05 November 2023

38608869R00090